Dreams
& Their
Meanings

Dreams & Their Meanings

TONY HAZZARD

WARD LOCK

A WARD LOCK BOOK

This edition published in the UK 1994
by Ward Lock
Wellington House
125 Strand
London
WC2R 0BB

A Cassell Imprint

Reprinted 1995

Copyright © Text and illustrations Ward Lock 1994

This book was previously published in 1989
(reprinted 1990, 1992)

Distributed in the United States
by Sterling Publishing Co., Inc.
387 Park Avenue South, New York, NY 10016-8810

Distributed in Australia
by Capricorn Link (Australia) Pty Ltd
2/13 Carrington Road, Castle Hill, NSW 2154

A British Library Cataloguing in Publication Data block for this
book may be obtained from the British Library

ISBN 0 7063 7324 3

Typeset by Columns of Reading Ltd
Printed and bound in Great Britain by
Biddles Ltd, Guildford and King's Lynn

CONTENTS

Introduction · 6
A Dreamer's A–Z · 32

INTRODUCTION
by Tony Hazzard

DREAMING YOUR LIFE AWAY

'All I have to do is dream' ... 'Dream Lover' ...
'Daydream' ... 'I'll see you in my dreams' ...
'Sweet dreams of you' ... 'Like dreamers do' ...
'I'm dreaming of a white Christmas' ... The list of
popular songs in which dreams and dreaming
feature is endless.

It illustrates just how deeply embedded in our
culture the power of dreams actually is – and the
extent to which we take it for granted without
question. But what are dreams, and what is
dreaming? Are they simply waste products of our
minds, discharged at night when the unconscious is
resting, so that we can face the next day without too
much psychological garbage getting in the way? Or
do they have a particular significance – should we
dismiss them as nonsense, or treat them with respect as
pointers to the future or as analyses of the past?

A character in Shakespeare's play *The Winter's
Tale* refers to dreams as 'toys'. In other words,
childish amusements of no importance. Yet the same
character goes on to describe a dream which has
clearly had a profound effect on him. Indeed,
Shakespeare's plays are full of references to dreams
and dreaming – he even based an entire play (*The
Tempest*) on a dream. It is clear that both the Bard
and his audiences attached great significance to
dreaming.

A deeper delve into the past, as we shall see,
reveals that dreams have played a significant role
since time began. But first let us take a look at some
of the types of dream you may experience in a
lifetime.

PROBLEM SOLVING DREAMS

In the Western world we tend to rely heavily on the value of reasoning. Scientific research is based on the power of deductive thinking. But it is by no means the only way of reaching a conclusion. How often have we heard the phrase 'Let's sleep on it', which shows clearly that, amid all the rational logic, part of us acknowledges the intuitive power of the unconscious to deal with a problem overnight.

There are many examples of solutions to problems arriving, like a gift from the gods, through the medium of dreams. In 1867, the Marquis Hervey de Saint-Denys in his book on dreams mentioned three prominent scientist-philosophers who gave credit to dreams for help in their work. One of them, French astronomer Jean Baptiste Biot, spoke about having done useful work in his sleep on several occasions.

In 1869, Russian chemist Dmitri Mendeleev, having attempted in vain to find a solution, went to bed one night and dreamed that he saw a table of the elements, in which 'they fell into place as required'. When he woke up he carefully recorded the dream and subsequently found that only one change was necessary to what later became known as the periodic table of the elements, a major development in science.

Author Brian Inglis records the remarkable case in 1883 of HV Hilprecht, Professor of Assyrian at the University of Pennsylvania. He had spent a long evening attempting to decipher two small fragments of what were supposed to be some Babylonian finger rings, from a hasty sketch made by someone who discovered them. Since one of the fragments appeared to have the letters KU inscribed on it, he guessed that it might be a reference to King Kurigalzu, but the other defeated him.

Tired and weary, he went to bed and was soon

asleep. Later, he described what happened: 'I dreamed the following remarkable dream. A tall, thin priest of the old pre-Christian Nippur, about forty years of age and clad in a simple abba, led me to the treasure chamber of the temple, on the south east side. He went with me into a small, low-ceilinged room without windows, in which there was a large wooden chest, while scraps of agate and lapis lazuli lay scattered on the floor . . .'

The priest went on to explain in minute detail the answer to the problem. Hilprecht related the dream to his wife as soon as he woke, in case he should later forget it. In the morning he examined the sketch and found he was able to read off the inscription.

There are many such reported cases in the 19th century, and similar dreams are still being experienced. American golfer Jack Nicklaus, for example, found that his play had slipped until 79 was his best round-the-course average. Then one night he had a dream about his golf swing. In the dream he was playing much better than usual, and realized that he was holding the club in a different way.

As he later told a golfing reporter: 'I was doing it perfectly in my sleep. So when I came to the course I tried it the way I did in my dream and it worked. I feel kind of foolish admitting it, but it really happened in a dream. All I had to do was change my grip just a little.'

INSPIRATIONAL DREAMS

These are dreams which give the germ of an idea to an artist, writer, creator, or inventor of some sort – often in the most vivid way. Robert Louis Stevenson's story of *Dr Jekyll and Mr Hyde* came to the author in a series of dreams: '. . . on the second night I dreamed the scene at the window, and a scene afterward in two in which Hyde, pursued for some crime, took the powder and underwent the change in the presence of his pursuers.'

Edgar Allan Poe encountered the subject of his favourite story *The Lady Ligeia* in a dream. While, in her journal of 1918, Katherine Mansfield wrote: 'I dreamed a short story last night, even down to its name, which was *Sun and Moon*. It was very light. I dreamed it all – about children. I got up at 6.30 and wrote a note or two because I knew it would fade. I'll send it sometime this week. It's so nice.'

Novelist Graham Greene also admitted that two of his novels began with a dream. He developed the strange knack of dreaming his characters' dreams instead of his own. 'That happened to me when I was writing *A Burnt Out Case*,' he recorded. 'The symbols, the memories, the associations of that dream belonged so clearly to my character Querry that next morning I could put the dream without change into the novel, where it bridged a gap in the narrative which for days I had been unable to cross.'

John Masefield's poem 'The Woman Speaks' came to him in a dream, too. He saw a tall woman dressed in furs and a picture hat. In the dream he knew of her past, and that she was in Lincoln's Inn Fields on a Sunday morning. As she gradually faded, 'the whole of the poem appeared in high relief on an oblong metal plate,' from which he wrote it down.

Dreams have proved endless sources of inspiration for artists. Gauguin dreamed of a Tahitian girl and reproduced her in a painting. William Blake's inspiration for writing, painting and engraving frequently came from dreams. In fact, his famous 'Songs of Innocence and Experience' would not have come into existence without the help of a dream. He was unknown, had no money, no chance of credit and consequently no means of publishing his work.

In a dream his dead brother Robert appeared to him and told him what to do. The next day his wife carried out the instructions and spent what little money they had on materials. The result was a series of poems and writings illustrated by colour plates which established a style of reproduction for which he subsequently became famous.

Many composers, too, have acknowledged the dream as their source of inspiration. Beethoven once dozed off on a long journey and dreamed he was in the Middle East, though he was in fact on his way to Vienna. During the dream he heard a piece of music which vanished from his memory as soon as he woke. However, on the return journey the next day, he fell asleep again and once more dreamed the elusive piece of music. This time he managed to remember it when he woke and committed it to manuscript, with only three small changes.

DREAMS OF SECOND SIGHT

Although such cases are fascinating, none are more so than those involving dreams of second sight and precognition. By second sight we mean the ability to see or know something that is taking place a great distance away, even hundreds or thousands of miles. Very often dreams involving second sight are concerned with some sort of disaster. The theory is that telepathy, or the transmitting of information from one mind to another, is the medium which conveys the information from the people involved in the disaster to others who are in some way 'tuned in'. The dream state seems to be a way of tuning in without realizing it.

A New York woman, for example, dreamed that her mother was in a lifeboat which was so overcrowded it was in danger of sinking. Next morning she told her husband who, seeing she was worried by it, reassured her that her mother was still in Europe – or so they both assumed.

The following day they read in the newspaper of the sinking of the *Titanic*. To their horror, her mother's name was on the passenger list. In the event, the woman survived. What is uncanny about the dream is that she had booked the voyage without telling her daughter. When she was in the overcrowded lifeboat she realized that it was very close to capsizing and that the end could not be far away. From that moment she thought long and hard about her daughter whom she believed she would never see again. The moment coincided exactly with the time of the daughter's dream.

Graham Greene also dreamed about the *Titanic* disaster on the night it happened, even though he was only five at the time. In 1921 he had another dream of a shipwreck, the newspaper report of which he didn't read until several days later. His dream occurred on a Saturday night and the sinking was reported as taking place a few minutes after midnight on that same Saturday.

Louis Heren, foreign editor of *The Times* in 1968, had been covering the American primaries when he had a terrible nightmare. 'Somebody was trying to assassinate Kennedy, and I was trying to defend him, swinging my portable typewriter,' he recalled 'I fell out of bed in a sweat. My wife comforted me and then went downstairs to make a pot of tea. She turned on the radio as the announcer was saying that Kennedy had been killed.'

Sometimes second sight dreams take place on a much smaller scale and are far less frightening. Such dreams are sometimes called *farewell dreams*, since the main part of the dream usually consists of a loved or related person saying goodbye to the dreamer at the time of death.

Theatre producer David Belasco recalled dreaming of his mother on the night she died. 'As I strove to speak and sit up she smiled at me a long reassuring smile, spoke my name – the name she called me in my boyhood – "Davy, Davy, Davy", then, leaning down, seemed to kiss me; then drew away a little and said: "Do not grieve. All is well and I am happy"; then moved toward the door and vanished.'

PRECOGNITIVE DREAMS

Again, these frequently involve disasters, but the times of dream and incident do not coincide. On the contrary, the dream precedes the incident. Many were recorded by JW Dunne in his book *An Experiment With Time*. One of his own dreams foretold the eruption of the volcano, Mount Pelee, in dramatic detail, which was later confirmed by newspaper reports.

Another form of precognitive dream is that of *déjà-vu* – the feeling of reliving an experience. In this case the experience has already been dreamed and is later lived out.

The late broadcaster Freddie Grisewood had a series of dreams when he was 12, which all featured a country house. His dreaming self was living in the house in Stuart times. Over a two week period he dreamed of riding over the rolling countryside.

Several years later, while staying with friends in Sussex, they took him to visit another friend who lived in the house of Grisewood's dreams. He was certain the house was the same one, the only difference being that the surrounding countryside was less wooded in reality. Not only was the exterior of the house the same, but he was able to identify parts of the interior, even down to the fact that a tapestry had been removed from a wall, a fact confirmed by his stunned hostess.

Comedian Roy Hudd, a great fan of music hall artist Dan Leno, also had a series of dreams about a house and its surroundings. What stood out in particular was the fact that the dream house seemed to be full of mirrors. Some time after, Roy and his wife came across the very house in an area of London they had never previously visited. Further investigation confirmed that the house had, in fact, contained several mirrors installed by one of its occupants, Dan Leno.

Although you may have had similar experiences of your own, the chances are that the majority of your dreams will tend to be much less exciting and probably far less easy to understand. Even non-existent, or perhaps so infrequent that you don't attach any importance to them. There are ways in which you can get more out of them. But first it is important to look at the story of dreams, and what modern research has taught us about them.

THE EARLIEST DREAMS

We know that dreams were being interpreted as far back as 2000 BC. An ancient Egyptian papyrus dating from the twelfth dynasty (1991–1786 BC) clearly records many interpretations of dreams. The Greek poet Homer, writing in the seventh century BC, uses a dream as a means of conveying a message from the gods. In fact, in the ancient world, dreams were commonly held to be the accepted medium through which the gods would speak.

In the *Old Testament* there are many famous examples of God speaking in dreams, from Jacob's dream of a ladder ascending to heaven to Joseph's well-known interpretation of Pharoah's dreams. Despite this wide acceptance of dreams as being of great significance, there was much debate about their true meaning and source.

Aristotle, the Greek philosopher, went against the ideas of his time and attributed the cause of dreams to nothing more than the impact of the physical, external world. In other words, sensory stimuli on the sleeper's body played the major part in forming the dream. If you dreamed of fire it was probably because you were too hot in bed. He also reasoned that, since the senses partially closed down in sleep, and the mind received fewer messages via the senses, the imagination tended to run riot with whatever sensory impressions got through.

The Roman statesman and writer Cicero (106–43 BC) published a forthright attack on dreams as a means of divination. Muhammed, the founder of the Muslim religion, even went so far as to ban the practice of divination through dreams. In his opinion it was becoming far too influential on daily life. But on the whole it was generally accepted that dreams were important enough to be recorded, investigated and interpreted.

In 700–600 BC the ancient Babylonians even published a forerunner of the book you are holding, a Babylonian 'dream-guide', discovered by archaeologists among the ruins of the city of Nineveh. The most famous dream guide was written in the second century AD by the Greek geographer Artemidorus. He called it *Oneirocritica*, from the Greek word *oneiros*, meaning a dream. Though how being a geographer qualified Artemidorus to write a dream guide we shall never know.

The ancients also used dreams, in conjunction with other methods such as animal sacrifices, to foretell the future and even heal the sick. In ancient Greece, dreams became directly associated with healing. Special temples were built where priests and priestesses were on hand to interpret dreams for the sick and suffering.

There are known to have been at least 600 such temples built in Greece, dedicated to Aesculapius, god of medicine. People would offer sacrifices to the god in the hope that he would appear to them in a dream, while they slept at night in the temple, and reveal how they might be cured.

In the Middle Ages the all-powerful church was the source of learning and knowledge, as well as wielding political power. Religious belief was accepted as the mainstay of life. But belief in God also ran alongside belief in the Devil. While folk paid lip service to Christianity they were not averse to dabbling in the fringes of religion. Astrology, necromancy, the Tarot and dream divination were all widely practised. Much of the literature of the time features the dream as the focal point. Chaucer's *Canterbury Tales*, Langland's *Piers Plowman*, and John Bunyan's *Pilgrim's Progress* all make use of dreams to weave their tales.

In the sixteenth century, philosophers turned their attention to dreams. The main question they asked was: 'How do I know that I'm not dreaming, even when I'm awake?' The conclusion centred around the idea that dreams cannot be linked through memory to the rest of our lives in the same way that real events are.

Despite such hard-nosed thinking, dreams continued to be tinged with the supernatural until the 1850s. A French doctor, Alfred Maury, reached the same conclusion as Aristotle, that dreams arose from external stimuli. One night he dreamed that he had been brought before a French revolutionary court, tried and condemned to execution by *guillotine*. As the blade fell he woke to find that part of his bed had fallen on the back of his neck.

He made a study of over 3,000 dreams to support his theory. Less than 50 years later Sigmund Freud, the founding father of modern psychiatry, published *The Interpretation of Dreams*, and paved the way for a whole new outlook.

THE DREAM MASTER

The work of Freud and Jung is very complex, but entirely changed the way we look at dreams today. Freud, who was born in 1856, described dreams as 'the royal road to the unconscious'. He believed that repressed urges and wishes express themselves in a disguised language through dreams.

What the dreamer remembers on waking is never the whole story. But, since the symbolic language of dreams tends to confuse us, we automatically try to make some order out of the chaos.

Freud discovered that some of the symbols were fixed and non-personal. In other words, they seemed to be archaic, unchanging, common to everyone, and not exclusive to dreams. They could be found in myths, fairy tales, art and religion. His conclusions provoked considerable controversy, along with many of his other theories.

Freud believed that myths, for example, were little more than thinly disguised fantasies that were common to all mankind. But the basic idea of symbols that were common the world over was shared by his most famous associate, Carl Gustav Jung. Jung, who was born in Switzerland in 1875, was 19 years younger than Freud. The two men later became working colleagues and close friends.

Whereas Freud saw dreams as a sort of valve through which the instinctive drives of the id (subconscious inherited impulses) could let off steam, Jung saw them as helpful guides to the psychic health of the individual. They offered useful advice as to how the person should be living his or her life.

HEROES AND VILLAINS

According to Jung, people became emotionally and neurotically ill when they veered away from their true path in life. The accompanying symptoms contained clues as to what might be done about it.

One of the clues is the archetypes which lie in the collective unconscious – the unconscious shared by all humanity. An archetype can best be described as a pattern, or tendency. Archetypes cannot be observed directly, but only by their influences – in the same way that a magnetic field can be discovered by its effects on iron filings.

An archetype is a tendency to structure images in a particular fashion, and these images are universal. This can be a difficult concept to grasp, but is very important with regard to Jung's view of dreams.

Archetypal images reflect important stages in human life, such as birth, marriage and death. They can be found in myths and fairy tales. Freud saw myths as fantasies, but Jung believed they described certain human situations, or ordeals on the journey through life. He also believed that some people tend to live according to the demands of an archetype.

One example of this is that of Puer, or Eternal Youth (*puer* is the Latin word for boy). He appears in the card deck as the Knave, in Piccadilly Circus as Eros, as Peter Pan, the boy who didn't want to grow up, in the images (as opposed to the real personality) of Cliff Richard, Michael Jackson or any other youthful pop star.

Puer is freewheeling, cannot be tied down, has many affairs but won't settle down to marriage. He is romantic, wild, always has hopes and plans which never materialize, lives dangerously, flies, parachutes, dies young. You get the picture?

Some young men in the grip of this archetype tend to follow quite distinct patterns as their lives unfold.

The same archetype may only manifest itself occasionally in the lives of others. Now these archetypal images may well appear in dreams, and Jung believed that it was helpful to identify them. This could then mean that the dreamer was being given a message from the wider arena of the collective unconscious. To interpret the dream simply on a personal level might be failing to get the whole story.

Archetypal images generally have a strong effect on us. They can be exploited by advertising and the media. If an image is guaranteed to influence a wide range of people, then it can be used to powerful effect.

In the film *ET*, the main character is an extraterrestrial who comes down from the sky, has extraordinary powers, heals the sick, dies and then comes back to life, after which he returns to his home in the sky. He is also extremely lovable.

This is a classic archetype image of the god who descends to earth, has a profound effect on people, but who dies and then is resurrected before ascending back to heaven. I'm sure the story has a familiar ring about it. It would not be wide of the mark to say that a major part of the film's success was due to the fact that the image and story are deeply embedded in the collective unconscious of human beings who will respond when that image is brought to life.

Another example of one of these archetypal figures is the Shadow – the part of ourselves that we don't want to acknowledge, for whatever reason. The Shadow usually appears as a dark person of the same sex as the dreamer. When he or she appears in a dream it can usually indicate a need for recognition. In other words, aspects of personality that have been locked away need to be brought out into the open. When this is done the person usually experiences a surge of energy and vitality.

Many of the Shadow's characteristics are derived from parental rules and restrictions. In order to please his parents, a young child will accentuate some and repress other behaviour.

For example, a child who is particularly gifted in some way may be scolded for displaying the talent too obviously — maybe it makes a brother or sister appear inadequate by comparison — so the child begins to hide his light under a bushel. This will then go to form shadow material. Later in life the shadowy figure may begin appearing in his dreams. It might well be an indication to the dreamer that the part of his personality repressed all those years ago wants to emerge. The dream may take on the aspect of a nightmare, with the shadow figure pursuing the dreamer.

Fear in dreams can often indicate simply that repressed contents are striving to emerge. Although the dream seems menacing, the purpose is anything but. The shadowy figure is urging the dreamer back on the path of individuation — becoming the person the dreamer really is. Instead of being like a car engine that is only firing on three cylinders, the dream is attempting to get the dreamer firing on all four cylinders.

When such images occur in dreams they can indicate that the dreamer has reached an important stage in life, or that the problems they are wrestling with in waking life have an archetypal connection.

It is necessary to explain all this because dreams and psychology have become inseparable. The greater our insight, the more fascinating our dreams become.

THE HEALING POWER OF DREAMS

Jung also found that dreams could be compensatory. In other words, some aspect lacking in the dreamer's life might appear to make up for its absence in waking life. This mechanism is a way of keeping the personality in balance, rather like the body's balancing mechanisms. When we get too hot, we begin to sweat, and this loss of liquid is in turn compensated by a feeling of thirst and the urge to drink in order to make up for the loss of body fluid.

Exactly the same process can occur in dreams, according to Jung. For example, if you've had an argument with a friend and become angry, your consideration for the friendship might over-rule your anger, which in turn might be suppressed. That night you may dream of being extremely angry. This is the unconscious finishing off in a more devious way the unfinished business of being angry which might otherwise upset the friendship.

If you have ever had recurring dreams, you may find it interesting that Jung believed that dreams also run in sequences. The unconscious makes the same point in a variety of ways. A series of dreams often gives a clearer picture than trying to interpret dreams in isolation.

Here's an example of the dreams of one of Jung's patients. He is a well-respected, self-made man with a scientific background who has risen from humble origins to a position of some importance. In his first dream he finds himself in a small village. He seems to be a very solemn figure in a long black coat. Under his arm he carries several books. There is a group of young boys whom he recognizes as former class mates from his school days. As he passes by he hears one of them comment that he (the dreamer) doesn't come this way much these days.

This dreamer came to see Jung because he appeared to have all the symptoms of mountain sickness, even though there appeared to be nothing organically wrong with him. In this first dream we have a clue as to the reason. The dreamer has risen too high too fast. He reminds Jung of a mountaineer who, having climbed 6,000 ft, sees another peak 12,000 ft above him and sets out to climb it, having forgotten that he is already tired from having climbed the first 6,000 ft. This, says Jung, accounts for the symptoms of mountain sickness. The comment of one of the boys in the dream indicates that he doesn't give much thought to his origins, to the life he has left behind.

The unconscious seemed determined to get its warning message through. In the next dream the man has to go to an important conference, but realizes that he has left it a bit late and must hurry. More haste means less speed, and he can't find his hat and coat. He rushes up and down the house in search of them. Finally he gets out of the house only to find that he has left behind some important papers. He rushes back for them, checking his watch.

As he runs to the station the road has become soft and boggy and his feet can hardly move. He arrives to find the train just leaving. His attention is drawn to the curve of the railway line. He realizes that if the engine driver doesn't slow down when the train reaches the bend, the rear carriages will be thrown off the line. The train gathers speed and the accident occurs as the dreamer wakes in panic.

Again the message is clear – he is going ahead too fast. He himself is the engine driver, driving his career, and heading for a breakdown, not seeing the things in the past, and in his unconscious. These are compensatory dreams, attempting to restore the inner life of the dreamer.

THE FRONTIERS OF DREAMS

In 1953 dream research entered a new era when it was noticed that the rapid movement of the eyes in sleep seemed to coincide with dreaming. The discovery was made by the simple process of waking the unfortunate subject when rapid eye movement — known as REM — was detected. On waking, the subject would report that he or she had been dreaming. A few months later it was observed that REM generally starts about an hour after falling asleep.

By means of an electroencephalograph — a machine for measuring electrical patterns produced by the brain — it was found that REM periods were accompanied by a change in brain wave patterns. The waves of a sleeping person in REM resembled someone fully awake and their breathing rate also increased. These episodes lasted between five and ten minutes, followed by quieter periods when the symptoms were absent. Then the cycle would repeat itself. This would happen three or four times a night.

Back in 1953, when volunteers were awakened during REM they reported vivid dreams 20 out of 27 times. When wakened during non-REM periods the incidence dropped to 4 out of 23. Since then thousands of experiments have been carried out along these lines and confirmed the original findings.

The conclusions are that vivid, visual dreams generally occur during REM periods. When woken in this state volunteers recall vivid dreams about 80 per cent of the time. Outside these periods the percentage falls to between 30 and 50 per cent. The dreams in this less active period tend to be more thoughtful, realistic and similar to waking life.

The D (for dream) state or rapid eye movement period takes up about 25 per cent of sleep time in young adults. Newborn babies spend 50 per cent of their sleep in the D state, while people in their sixties show a slight lessening of the D state.

D state sleep has been observed in all mammals, including dogs, cats, monkeys, elephants, shrews and opossums. Even birds and reptiles have shown some evidence of it. Investigations have shown that the D state is centred round an area of the brain stem and involves a chemical produced by the body called norepinephrine. In addition, various changes take place in the body, such as changes in heart and breathing rates and reductions in the electrical activity of certain muscles.

Another interesting fact emerged from the studies. When people were deprived of D state sleep they would compensate at the first opportunity by dreaming even more. Not only that, but they would dream more during the following nights, as if to replenish their depleted stock of dream material. In fact, sleep and dream deprivation have been used as a method of torture. The subject will become anxious and tense and will start to hallucinate.

Most people can manage on far less sleep than they might believe. You can train yourself to do this by gradually decreasing the amount of sleep each night. The body and mind soon seem to accept the new regime and compensate accordingly. In other words, less sleep produces deeper sleep. Those who normally need eight hours or more find they can make do with five or six hours. What they cannot do without is D state sleep.

So it would appear that we have a very real need to dream. 'But', you might say, 'that can't possibly apply to me, because I don't dream.' Wrong. Evidence suggests that we all dream, but that some of us recall better than others.

During the D states that occur towards the end of sleep people tend to wake automatically about 40 per cent of the time, and thus recall the fact that they were dreaming. This figure tallies with those who say they remember their dreams.

Another relevant factor is how important it is to

remember dreams. For the majority of us it's of little importance whether we remember them or not, but it is possible to increase dream recall deliberately.

Sleep researchers have found that external stimuli have little bearing on dream content. Talking to someone, or gently prodding them during the D state will not necessarily be reflected in their dreams. Obviously there are exceptions, and most people have experienced dreams of passing water coinciding with a strong urge to do so on waking.

In addition to the D state there are another two states which occur as one begins to fall asleep and as one start to wake up. During these periods the semi-sleeper enters a dream-like state half way between waking and sleeping when what might be described as vivid daydreams occur. During these times REM does not take place, but the semi-sleeper may feel that he or she is actually dreaming. The main difference is that such 'dreamlets' tend to be less emotional, less complicated and more fleeting.

Now these scientific tests are all very well, but they bring us no nearer to capturing our own dreams so that we can interpret and examine them.

TIPS FOR THE DREAM-CATCHER

First of all you may say, 'I don't dream.' But as we've seen, what you are really saying is, 'I never remember my dreams.' If this is the case, then the first thing to do is to give your unconscious some encouragement. You can do this by keeping a notepad and pen by the bed. It may act as a stimulus to your memory and may help to wake you up at the appropriate time. The next thing to do is to tell yourself very firmly: 'Tonight I am going to remember my dream as soon as I wake up.' Or even better: 'I shall wake up at the end of my first dream.' Don't despair if you don't have immediate success.

The next bit is the hardest. If you manage to wake up in the middle of the night immediately after a dream, *you must put on the light and write the dream down straight away.* What tends to happen at 3.30am is that you wake up, and think that you've had a dream which is so vivid that you're convinced you'll remember it in the morning. Not so. The chances are, the sleep in between will erase it from your memory.

Once the system begins to work, and you're so exhausted each morning from spending the entire night writing out dreams, it's a good idea to record the dreams in a more permanent dream journal. There are several reasons for this. One is to achieve some form of continuity. This is essential for interpretation, as dream images may reappear continually and may gradually change. A permanent record can help to give a clear idea of the frequency and change of repeated dream images.

In addition, dreams on the whole tend not to make much sense on first examination. Sometimes this is due to the time sequence involved. If the dream is saying something about the way you're living your life, you may find that your unconscious is anticipating your conscious mind by several months, and the dream may start to make sense after a few months have elapsed. A dream journal can also show clearly the link between apparently unconnected dreams, where several images are used in a sequence of very different dreams, which are all giving the same message. Such reinforcement through varying images may help to throw light on dreams which have otherwise seemed obscure. Also, if you can see that there is, after all, a definite message appearing repeatedly in a series of dreams, then only by re-reading your journal can you 'get the message' and possibly act on it.

So, having remembered and recorded your dreams, what can you do with them? Well, one thing is just learn to live with them. That's not as strange as it sounds. Our Western, analytical society sets great store by investigating, dissecting and generally getting to the bottom of the world, both around us and within us, and jolly useful it is, too. But other cultures sometimes do things slightly differently. North American Indians or Australian Aborigines would tend to look on dreams as very important gifts which should be treated with reverence.

A dream of a panther is, they might say, a gift from the gods. Rather than trying to find out what it 'means' they would suggest meditating on it, even treating it as real. In fact, this attitude can also be useful if you want to get more out of the dream. Because the dream comes from the unconscious, it is sometimes helpful to utilize methods which use the power of the unconscious. You can *amplify* a dream image by immersing yourself in it. If you dream of a panther, for example, try drawing it; writing about it; looking at pictures of panthers; best of all, go and see a real one in a zoo. What is it trying to say to you? Does it want something from you? Can you be of help to it in any way?

Such questions are useful when one applies the technique of *creative visualization*, a method used by Jung. Another name for it is the 'waking dream'. It can be used in all sorts of ways and for all sorts of purposes. In this case we can use it to find out what a dream image means or even to go back into a dream and continue it. To do this you need to relax, either by sitting comfortably in a chair, or by lying on the floor. Use whatever relaxation techniques suit you best, relaxing your muscles one by one, or concentrating on steady, even breathing. When you're fully relaxed, imagine that you're back in your dream. This time you have rather more control. Visualize the scene as you remember it.

Take your time. Then, when you're ready, ask the main character, image, or group of characters if they have any message for you, or if you can be of help to them, or even why they are acting the way they are. Don't try and force an answer. Just allow it to happen. It may not come from the dream image or the characters: it may come in the form of a sound, or visually, or as a word. Some people are better at this technique than others, so don't worry if it doesn't work for you. If you have a very strong imagination or are of a nervous disposition it might be more sensible to use a more down-to-earth technique which doesn't stimulate the imagination so much. In any event, give yourself time to come back 'down to earth' at the end of the session.

A good way of doing this is to open your eyes and when you're ready take a good long look at the contents of the room around you. It might help to describe them to yourself out loud. This reorientation is very important. It might also help to conduct a visualization session with others, so that you can all help each other, either through questions, guidance through the dream, or reorienting afterwards.

A simpler technique is derived from Gestalt therapy. Describe the dream out loud in your own words, but make sure you use the present tense throughout, e.g. 'I'm in a long corridor which seems to disappear in the distance. Suddenly a woman appears and asks me if I'd like an orange, which she holds out to me. I take it and as I do so it begins to change into a frog . . .' Do this three times. Again, it's helpful to do this with someone else. They can act as observer for you and notice any changes.

The reason for repeating it three times is that very often the second or third repeats throw up more details which didn't emerge in the first account. Also, repeating it can sometimes give you an insight as to its meaning. When you've done that, repeat the process all over again, but this time from another point of view. This can belong to any other person or object in the dream. For example: 'I'm in a long corridor and I seem to disappear into the distance. Inside me is (here say your name) and a woman . . .' Note if any of the phrases could apply to your own personality. Do you tend to disappear into the distance when people are talking to you, leaving them centre stage? Remember how the unconscious works by associations and puns sometimes. This technique works on the principle that all the different parts of the dream are various aspects of the dreamer's own personality. It can be surprisingly revealing.

Although the following dictionary of symbols will give you the traditional meanings of dream images used down the ages, it's worth noting certain major ones.

SOME IMPORTANT SYMBOLS

HOUSE   This is generally taken to represent the psyche of the dreamer. Sometimes the house will feel familiar but the dreamer will suddenly come across some additional rooms that he didn't expect. This usually refers to aspects of the dreamer's personality that have been hidden away or unexplored.

Particular rooms can have additional meanings. Kitchens are where ingredients are 'transformed' into food. A dream which features the kitchen could indicate some sort of change within the dreamer's personality. Bathrooms can be places where old things can be washed away or eliminated, and so on.

SEX Dreams of sexual intercourse are very common and can be attributed to unsatisfied sexual urges which seek expression in the dream. But sometimes dreams of intercourse, especially without any accompanying sexual excitement, can be symbolic of a union of some sort, a joining together or an alliance between different parts of the dreamer's personality. A man dreamed of being in bed with his brother and being erotically attracted to him, although in waking life he was heterosexual. The dream signified that, despite the very real differences between the two men, the dreamer needed to unite with certain aspects of his brother's personality, in other words take on some of those aspects. The dreamer was a sensitive, thoughtful man, who tended to take other people's wishes into account at the expense of himself, whereas the brother was quite ruthless and unfeeling with regard to others. The unconscious was hinting that some of that ruthlessness was needed to stop other people taking advantage of the dreamer.

DEATH Many people are worried by dreams of death, but there is no need to be. Dreams of death are usually concerned with change or transformation. The death in the dream will most probably refer to a change that is taking place within the dreamer's personality. There may be accompanying anxiety but this is because the ego always dislikes change and will try to fight it. Death dreams often accompany exciting changes in one's real life. Unconscious knowledge of impending death in, for example, a person who is terminally ill, maybe without consciously knowing it, will usually produce a completely different dream: sometimes a journey, or a move or a change of some sort. The unconscious mind seems to be less alarmed by death than the conscious ego.

TRANSPORT and JOURNEYS These usually refer to our journey through life and the way in which we're proceeding. Are we in control of the transport? Are we going too fast? Have we taken a wrong turning? Are we in a train, a car, or a bus? Trains can sometimes imply rigidity of lifestyle, since they run on fixed rails without being able to turn off at will. Are we flying too high in a plane? Will we crash or break down if we continue in the same way? Such questions can all be applied to dreams of travel and show how words can mean so many different things depending on the context. Cars break down, but so do people. Are we up in the clouds? Our language is so full of imagery which we take for granted until the unconscious uses it to give us a message.

WATER Water in dreams is generally taken to refer to two main areas: the unconscious and the emotions. Diving down under water usually refers to diving down into the unconscious, whereas an anxiety dream involving rising water levels can refer to the dreamer's fear of being swamped by uncontrollable emotions. The latter dream would probably be dreamed by someone who was calm and rational on the surface (yet another image) but was unconsciously aware of strong emotions underneath.

When trying to unravel the meaning of a dream it may be helpful to remember the following:

People and objects in dreams should always be considered in relation to the dreamer. If you're trying to help someone else unravel the meaning of their dream, always ask them what a particular dream image means to them. This can be of great significance.

One dreamer described a dream in which she was having tea with Queen Elizabeth, the Queen Mother.

Many people would pounce on this image and say something like, 'This person feels insignificant and her unconscious is trying to boost her morale,' or 'She has a great sense of her own importance.' In this case they would be wide of the mark, for this particular dreamer had spent many happy hours in her childhood in Scotland having tea at Balmoral with the Queen Mother: it had a very different meaning for her than it would for most of us.

The following words, by a Jungian analyst, beautifully sum up the nature of dreams: 'Dreams are mysterious entities, like messages from an unknown friend who is caring but objective. The handwriting and the language are at times obscure, but there is never any doubt as to the underlying concern for our ultimate welfare – which may be different from the state of well-being that we imagine to be our goal.'

But let us allow Luis Buñuel, the dream-inspired film director, to have the last word: 'If someone were to tell me I had twenty years left and asked me how I'd like to spend them, I'd reply: "Give me two hours a day of activity and I'll take the other twenty-two in dreams."'

Happy dreaming.

A DREAMER'S A-Z

A

ABANDON If you abandon someone in a dream take care; it could be a warning to avoid trouble. Witnessing an abandonment can mean there is important news in the offing. As in all dreams, your own specific circumstances must be considered first. For example, if you are leaving home a dream of abandonment can merely be anxiety or anticipation about becoming independent. It can also be the preliminary to a reconciliation or a recovery from trouble.

ABROAD If you dreamt you were in a foreign country you are probably generally unsettled. The dream may point to a change of location or lifestyle. Travelling abroad by ship predicts a new influential friendship.

ABYSS The most important question is – did you avoid the fall? If so, you will overcome difficulties ahead. If, however, you fell take it as a warning and be extremely careful in any business dealings.

ACCIDENT This kind of dream can generally be interpreted as an unfortunate omen. Avoid the cause of the accident in the dream and take precautions for a few days. An accident at sea can often indicate a storm in your love life.

ADULTERY If you committed adultery in the dream, be on your guard and keep your own counsel, particularly in sharing confidences with new friends. Resistance to temptation of this kind indicates a happy and successful life. There may be disappointing set-backs, but they will only be temporary.

AFRAID Another dream of contrary, suggesting that you will find the courage of your convictions, your cause will succeed or your lover will be faithful.

AGE To dream of worrying about your age indicates a potential illness. Monitor your health and, if necessary, consult a doctor. A dream peopled with elderly folk, on the other hand, is an omen of good luck. If they are needy, however, there may be difficulties ahead. To overcome them you must be positive and strong.

ANGER Anger against a person you know indicates that they are a good friend to you. If the cause or object of your anger was unknown there may be good news on its way.

ANIMALS The interpretation of animals in a dream must depend upon the dreamer's attitudes, instincts and individual circumstances. Traditional interpretations are very general, for example, wild animals indicate your affairs will prosper. If the animals are menacing or aggressive there may be reversals of fortune and trouble ahead. Baby animals indicate children, immaturity or vulnerability. Animals with cubs denote motherliness. If you have an animal, or are afraid of them, traditional dream interpretations may not apply to your specific circumstances. Individual animals are listed under their names.

ANKLE A dream in which an ankle is featured may predict that a solution will be found or success will ensue after initial difficulties. Ankles of the opposite sex can indicate an unwise romance.

ANTS If they were portrayed as industrious creatures then think about a change in your career or position. As pests in your dream they forecast a period of frustration and hard work.

APPETITE A subject open to various interpretations, and one in which the dreamer must take into account his or her individual circumstances. Hunger or thirst can indicate sexual desire clothed by the dreamer in a more acceptable form. However, hunger or loss of appetite could signify health troubles. Sharing a meal with someone can mean a wish for closer intimacy with them. An insatiable appetite usually refers to finances – handle your money carefully; don't spend it all at once.

APPLES Fruit is generally a good omen of success and rewards in life. Sour apples indicate that you will be responsible for some loss or misfortune.

ARROW If you dream that someone shoots an arrow at you, beware of a friend or associate who will let you down or may be working against your interests. A broken arrow symbolizes a relationship you would do best to end.

ASCENDING Going upwards in a dream denotes success. To reach the top of a hill means the overcoming of obstacles and the eventual realization of your ambitions.

AUDIENCE Were you performing for an audience? If so, there is a distinction or happy social occasion on its way. If you were in the audience there will be good news for a friend.

AVALANCHE Being caught in an avalanche traditionally means you will have a surprising stroke of good luck. If others were caught it foretells a change of surroundings. The presence of an avalanche in your dreams generally indicates obstacles and problems in your path.

B

BABY Many babies indicate happiness, fulfilment and satisfaction. A pretty baby signifies helpful friends. If you were unhappy with the baby in your dream, beware of a treacherous friend. A helpless or sick baby is a warning of approaching difficulties in business or your personal life.

BACK DOOR Using the back door instead of the front indicates important changes ahead. Strangers or burglars at your back door is a dream of contrary and signifies a windfall of money on its way to you. If friends used your back door in your dreams be wary of any suggested new ventures.

BADGER A good omen of success and prosperity through your own efforts.

BAKING A dream about baking indicates a rise in status or a financial boost. *See also* Bread.

BALL If you enjoyed dancing at the ball, the dream is a happy omen of pleasant times to come. A masked ball is a warning of false friends.

BALL GAMES Unless related to your daytime activities, a dream involving ball games generally signifies happy news.

BALLOON A number of toy balloons foretells trivial problems or disappointments. A large balloon rising predicts some happy achievement; though a descending balloon indicates setbacks.

BANDAGE A dream of contrary. A bandage signifies good influences around you – not an accident, as you might expect.

BAREFOOT Finding yourself barefoot in a dream indicates difficulties to overcome before arriving at your goal. To be completely naked is a lucky omen.

BARN A barn in a good condition signifies prosperity. An empty or derelict barn warns against risky investment.

BASIN A full basin indicates family or romantic problems. An empty basin can be taken as a good omen. If you were eating or drinking from a basin in the dream, there will be difficulties in love and, according to old sources, it is probable that you will not marry your first love.

BATHING Bathing dreams are very specific. Did you dream of an empty bath, for instance? Then re-think any decisions you have recently made – you could be wrong. If the water was too hot or too cold, you may have to revise or alter your plans. A pleasantly warm bath, however, is a good omen. If you were bathing in the sea in your dream, then prepare yourself for some astonishingly good luck. Bathing in a river indicates a joyful surprise ahead, though bathing in a lake warns of difficulties. Bathing with friends might mean that an approach for help is on the way.

BEAR A bear in your dream generally indicates a struggle before you achieve success. Killing off a bear suggests triumph over opposition.

BED To dream of being in your bed traditionally signifies security. A strange bed is a sign of good fortune in business or career. If you were making a bed in your dream be prepared for visitors or a change of residence.

BEES Buzzing bees bring good news to the dreamer. Bees generally indicate that your own industry will be rewarded. A beehive signifies dignity and honour, though an empty beehive may warn of financial problems ahead. Dead or listless bees suggest you should use more discretion in choosing friends – be careful with your confidences.

BEREAVEMENT A dream of contrary predicting news of a birth, wedding or an engagement.

BICYCLE In dreams the bicycle is interpreted as a symbol of assistance. It is necessary to consider its appearance and condition; whether you were on the flat or going up or down hill. Was the road clear, was the weather good or bad, and so on.

BIRDS Despite Alfred Hitchcock, flying birds are usually a good omen, indicating an upturn in your circumstances. If you are already wealthy they may signify setbacks. Singing birds augur well for the dreamer, while birds with brightly coloured plumage, who are not afraid of you, predict an elevation in status and influence. Injured or dead birds forecast worries on the way, but if they are birds of prey, any problems will be short-lived.

BIRTH For anyone expecting a baby there is no significance attached to dreaming about births. Generally, however, a dream about the birth of a child predicts good news to come. Multiple births signify an upturn in finances. Animal births indicate that you will succeed over opposition.

BLIND Blindness in a dream, whether your own sight-loss or that of others, is a direct warning to be on your guard against deceit – even among those closest to you. Review your 'friends' closely.

BLUNDER If you dream of blundering around, don't worry. This is a dream of contrary which signifies that you will do very well in your ventures.

BREAK Broken articles generally indicate problems. More specifically, broken furniture signifies insolvency; if you break a looking glass you may hear of a death; and if windows are broken take it as a warning to guard against robbery and fire. Two exceptions are spectacles which if broken indicate success, and bones which if fractured can forecast a surprise legacy.

BRIDGE A bridge in your dream means changes on the way. If the bridge was in good repair and you crossed without difficulty, look forward to improved prospects or financial advancement. A damaged or gloomy looking bridge is a warning – the grass may not be greener on the other side. Be cautious about making changes.

BUILDINGS Dream buildings represent your achievements in life. Therefore the condition and situation can be of great importance. Generally, the bigger and better the building the more prosperity you can look forward to. The more dilapidated the building the poorer you may become, unless you try to improve your prospects. A happy, cosy cottage signifies contentment, peace and comfort but not great wealth ahead of you.

BURIAL A dream of contrary predicting news of a wedding or a birth. A nightmare of being buried alive, however, warns against involvement in shady deals. It may also indicate that the dreamer is in an unhappy relationship in which he or she feels dominated or smothered.

BUTTER Any dream in which butter is involved is a good omen, so look forward to some good fortune and a secure future.

C

CAGE An empty cage with an open door signifies an elopement, jilting or lost opportunity. A cage full of birds indicates a solution to your money worries, perhaps even an inheritance. Two birds in a cage predict a happy relationship.

CANAL In all dreams concerning water the condition of the water is important. Clean, clear water is a good omen, whereas muddy or murky water predicts trouble on the way. Weeds in a canal warn of carelessness with money, while canal locks represent an untrustworthy 'friend'.

CANDLE A brightly burning candle is a good sign but if the candle was not lit or was snuffed out be prepared for disappointment, trouble or news of a death. Carrying or buying candles or candlesticks indicates a happy social event in the offing. Short candles or flickering flames signify opportunity or change.

CARPET If the carpet featured in your dream was rich and colourful, congratulations: it is a good omen indicating a bout of good luck, advancement and financial prosperity. A shabby, worn or faded carpet is a warning to review your finances and to stay out of debt.

CASTLE A ruined or derelict castle denotes too much passion and bad temper in the dreamer. If the castle was in good repair and habitable it signifies a change of scenery, or a secure future.

CATS An unfavourable dream denoting deceit and treachery. Be very careful whom you trust; it is also a sign to single men and women that their lover is not what she or he seems to be. If you kill a cat in your dream it signifies that you will discover and overcome those against you. If you chase or scare off a cat then some good luck is in the offing.

CEMENT If cement featured in your dream – in whatever way it was used – it is a lucky omen for advancement or a rise in income.

CHAIR If you dream of an empty chair expect to hear news from a distant friend or relative. A rocking chair denotes a surprise bonus or gain through another person.

CHICKENS Traditionally, to dream of a hen and chickens predicted a bad season for the farmer. If the dreamer has no farming connections, chickens in a dream indicate that the dreamer is counting his or her chickens before they hatch.

CHIMNEY If your dream chimney was tall and well built it is a sign of successful achievement. An average chimney is a good, though not great, portent. A smoking chimney means good news is coming, though sparks from a chimney are a warning for you to use more tact and discretion. A cracked or broken chimney implies problems. A tumbledown chimney predicts a celebration.

CHINA A happy omen signifying a period of plenty and comfort in family affairs. Cracked or broken china indicates a change which you will be reluctant to accept but which will turn out well in the end.

CHURCH If your dream featured the outside of the church then it is a lucky omen. In dreaming of all sacred buildings the exterior is considered as fortunate but the interior denotes minor troubles on the way. To dream of a churchyard signifies better, even good times ahead.

CLERGY Like the inside of a church, clergy are never a fortunate omen and usually signify impending disappointment.

CLOCK Hearing a clock strike in your dreams traditionally predicts a speedy marriage and a comfortable life. Noticing or hearing a clock ticking is taken as a warning to use your time more positively.

CLOTHES To dream of having lots of clothes is a dream of contrary – so the more clothes you had in your dream the more you must prepare for worries ahead. Dreaming of a lack of clothes, being only partly dressed or, especially, being naked predicts good fortune, probably financial. The less clothing you had the better the circumstances to come. Dreaming of dressing can denote some success ahead, while undressing in a dream foretells of problems and reverses.

CLUMSINESS A dream of contrary indicating that the greater your clumsiness the more capable you will be in dealing with problems and sensitive situations that may arise. Dreaming of clumsiness in others denotes the possibility of some new and interesting people in your life.

COBWEBS If you dreamt of cobwebs which you brushed aside, then you will overcome any problems ahead. Look out for hidden opponents or competitors for you should easily outwit them. Dreaming of cobwebs in attics or other dark places signifies a period of good luck.

COLOURS Gay and bright colours in your dream signify security and success for the dreamer. Coloured flags and banners streaming in the air denote honour and esteem ahead. Occasionally a particular colour may dominate a dream – white promises success, especially in matters involving other people or the public; black can be unfavourable, unless it is connected with mourning, in which case it predicts your triumph over problems, and eventual success. Blue suggests that you will overcome worries, probably with some help; yellow also predicts some reverses before advancement can be made. Grey and orange indicate a waiting period and delays. Shades of lilac forecast temporary unhappiness or disappointment. Purple is a good omen, predicting happy social events; green signifies travel or news from afar; brown is lucky for finances and pink denotes unusual success. Bright red is a warning to keep control of your temper and deep red is the forerunner of good news.

CONFETTI If you dreamt of confetti then be prepared to celebrate: your social success is assured.

COOKING A fortunate dream relating to material comforts whether you were or someone else was actually doing the cooking.

COSTUME A dream in which you or someone else was wearing costume or fancy dress signifies some extraordinary happenings or amazing news.

CROSSROADS This is a straightforward symbol indicating that there is an important decision on your horizon. Keep an open mind, listen to advice but make your own judgement.

CRYING This is usually an indication that someone you know needs your sympathy and understanding. If, however, it was a baby's cry then some good news is on its way.

D

DAGGER A dagger or a knife in your dream implies a letter or news from afar. If you were carrying a dagger then discretion is needed to avoid confrontation and trouble. Others with daggers or someone being stabbed by a dagger signifies opposition which you can, and will, overcome.

DANCING A positive dream signifying new friends and good times ahead. If you were dancing then your plans will succeed. Romance will be favoured.

DANGER A dream warning of difficulties ahead. Physical danger suggests that you must look after your health. If you avoided the danger in your dream then you can expect some difficulties. If you faced up to, or coped with, the danger then you are capable of success – go for it.

DARKNESS This indicates reversals and problems. If you made your way to the light then your difficulties will be temporary. If you dreamt that you were walking in the dark, you will find something you thought you had lost.

DEATH This is a rare dream and the interpretation of it is almost the exact opposite to the dream itself. If you were dead then you may look forward to a recovery from illness or anxiety. Death in a dream often predicts news of a birth, unexpected inheritance or a lucky windfall.

DESERTION If you dreamed that you deserted someone, then steer clear of gossip or you could lose a friend. If you were deserted then you may be confident that your friends are loyal and sincere.

DICE If you dreamt that you had a run of luck you may expect a modest gain. Dice, however, are a symbol of risk and generally apply to your lifestyle. Are you contemplating an affair? If so you may stand to lose more than you will gain. Are you chasing financial success? Then slow down to avoid putting what you already have in jeopardy. Take some time to consolidate your assets and position.

DIRT To dream that you or your clothes are dirty denotes poor health, sorrow or a loss of virtue, a warning you would do well to take heed of. If the dirt was thrown at you, beware of someone in whom you are confiding: they may try to injure your reputation. Stepping or falling into a rubbish pile traditionally means there is a happy change of address in the offing.

DISTRESS Oddly enough, this is a fortunate omen, whether the distress affected you or others. An expected loss will turn into a gain for you.

DITCH An unfavourable dream – the ditch symbolizes obstacles and problems. Traditionally it is a warning against a romantic attachment which could lead to an unhappy marriage. It is also a sign of enemies in your path; if you are in business take steps to avoid severe financial pitfalls.

DIVORCE For a married person this is a dream of contrary, signifying fidelity and security in their marriage. A single person, however, should look upon this dream as a warning to ensure that the object of their affections is worthy of them.

DOG The dog is generally recognized as a symbol of friendship and indicates happy times in good company. If a dog barks in recognition it is a sign of enjoyable social events ahead. A menacing or warning bark indicates possible legal wrangles or inconvenience – better check you have a TV licence. Fighting dogs represent friends in dispute: use discretion if you are involved. A dog which snarls, bites or attacks you implies that you have an untrustworthy friend.

DOOR An open door, especially one leading to sunshine or a pleasant view, is a good omen of success. If there is more than one open door then there are various opportunities open to you. Closed or locked doors, however, imply lost opportunities, or regrets. Don't waste any more time worrying about them.

DOVES Doves are usually a fortunate omen predicting a happy family life, good friends, prosperity in business and peaceful prospects. Cooing doves imply mutual love in any romantic relationship. Beware of the sound of the turtle-dove, if you can recognize it, for traditionally it is a warning of the death of a friend. A flock of doves in your dream signifies some news from a distance or even some unexpected travel.

DRAGON A dragon in your dream is a lucky sign of power and influence, probably representing a person who will be of great benefit to you in your career or financial prospects.

DRINK The significance of any drink depends upon its appearance and taste. A refreshing drink such as cool, clear water is always a good omen though discoloured or murky water denotes approaching trouble. If you are thirsty and cannot obtain a drink, then watch out for trials ahead which you may have to bear without assistance. Cultivate some self-reliance. To dream that you supplied someone else with a drink suggests that you are a sympathetic person. Wine, lemonade and party drinks predict happy and exciting times. Alcohol in moderation signifies success, while too much indicates indiscretion and embarrassment, which you may be called to account for.

DUMB Dreaming of yourself or someone else being dumb is a warning against giving away confidences or unwise speculation. If you wish to avoid embarrassment, steer clear of business and financial risks and keep your own counsel for a while.

DUNGEON If you were in the dungeon and couldn't escape, then it is a warning of obstacles too great for you to overcome; re-think your plans. If you do escape, then the dream implies you will overcome reversals and eventually your plans will come to fruition.

DUST A symbol of petty problems. If you wiped away the dust then this annoying phase will only be temporary. A dust cloud is a warning of trouble ahead which will need a good deal of clearing up.

DWARF A lucky omen, unless there was something wrong with the dwarf, in which case take stock of your friends: one of them may be false.

DYE The significance of this dream depends upon the details and atmosphere. If you were changing your hair colour out of vanity, then take care not to place yourself in a foolish position. If, however, you were merely enjoying a change, the dream implies some career success due to your own creative initiative. Dyeing garments denotes success in the personal and social spheres. Dyeing anything black, however, indicates sadness, perhaps over a broken relationship.

E

EAGLE An eagle perched on a mountain top indicates that you will reach the pinnacle of your ambition. A soaring eagle signifies advancement to your highest hopes in business or career. This magnificent bird is nearly always an omen of success, even fame, in the life of the dreamer. An attacking, angry eagle forecasts obstacles in your path which you must strive to overcome in order to achieve the recognition you deserve.

EARWIG An unfortunate dream as the earwig represents a rival in affairs of the heart. Be warned and on your guard, as your enemy may work in secret and threaten your happiness and prosperity.

EATING To dream of eating with others signifies good company and financial security. Eating alone is not a good sign, indicating quarrels or separation, reversals in income or status. Occasionally a specific food features in a dream, and may have a particular significance, e.g:

Almonds – good luck, but if they were bitter tasting, beware of making changes just now.

Apples – *see under* **APPLES**.

Apricot – luck in everything except love.

Artichoke – troubles with the opposite sex.

Asparagus – depend upon your own judgement and push ahead if your plans are to be fulfilled.

Bacon – tasty bacon implies continuing comfort; rancid bacon is a warning to look after your health.

Banana – a period of hard work ahead with small reward.

Beef – if you enjoyed a helping of beef look forward to an upturn in your business or career.

Berries – comforts, but not riches, on the horizon.
Biscuits – petty problems, temporary separation.
Blackberries – caution: financial austerity ahead.
Cake – a lucky omen.
Carrots – unexpected money.
Cauliflower – lucky omen, more of life's comforts ahead.
Celery – happiness and abundance.
Cheese – romantic pleasures.
Chips – potato chips indicate an improvement in your personal life.
Chocolate – good health and contentment.
Crackers – a domestic quarrel in the offing.
Dates – news of a marriage, not necessarily your own.
Drumsticks – omen of good luck.
Dumplings – a release from anxiety.
Eggs – good health or improvement in health.
Endive – an interesting foreigner or foreign place on your horizon.
Figs – unexpected news, probably from a distance.
Fish – generally a good omen.
Fruit – *see under* specific fruits.
Garlic – a fortunate omen except for those who detest it.
Gingerbread – a family celebration in the offing.
Grapes – do not be too preoccupied with luxury and the opposite sex.
Gruel – do not associate with heavy drinkers: they will drag you down.
Ham – good fortune in business.
Hazelnuts – discussions could turn into quarrels.
Herring – fish are always a good omen, and can indicate success in work after much diligent effort.
Honey – a good sign of plenty and rewards for your industry.
Jelly – difficulties to overcome.

Leeks – continuous effort may pay off.

Lemon – disappointment in love, family tiffs or an embarrassing predicament.

Meat – *see* Beef.

Melon – hopefulness; change for the better.

Mushrooms – important social contacts.

Mustard – reward for your labours, good news.

Oranges – problems at work.

Oysters – hard work ahead.

Pancakes – help from a friend will lead to some unexpected success.

Parsley – good luck and success, but, as with all green vegetables, only after some hard labour.

Peaches – small joys in store.

Peanuts – many friends.

Pears – juicy gossip.

Peas – prosperity.

Peppermint – unexpected windfall.

Pheasant – good financial prospects, maybe a new job.

Pineapple – convivial company, upturn in your social life.

Plums – respect and recognition for your diligence.

Popcorn – good health and romance.

Pork – prosperity, plenty.

Potatoes – comfort, contentment, modest needs.

Pudding – you have sufficient for your needs in life.

Radishes – domestic tiffs.

Raisins – overspending could get you into trouble.

Raspberries – good for romance.

Salad – your many talents are recognized.

Sausage – a mixed bag, domestic upsets, minor health problems.

Soup – a good omen, financial gain.

Strawberries – *see* Raspberries.

Sugar – a good omen: you have a harmonious period ahead.

Tapioca – small losses.
Tomatoes – a favourable sign. *See also* **TOMATOES**.
Turkey – disruption in relationships.
Vegetables – you must expend a great deal of energy before you may reap the rewards of your labour.
Watercress – romantic and domestic upsets.

EAVESDROPPING To dream that someone was eavesdropping is a warning that you may soon find yourself in a situation which is difficult to handle. If you were the eavesdropper then there will be some surprising good luck in store for you.

EGGS Dreaming of eggs in a nest predicts an unexpected windfall of money. Brightly coloured eggs or Easter eggs traditionally denote a celebration. To dream of seeing a number of eggs augurs well for business and love affairs, but broken or stale eggs warn of false friends and disappointments.

EMBARRASSMENT A dream of contrary which bodes well for the dreamer. The more embarrassed you felt the greater the respect, admiration and appreciation you may receive. If others were embarrassed in your dream, it is a warning for you to rely on your own judgement.

EMBROIDERY To observe embroidery or to see someone embroidering in your dream indicates deceit in a person you trust. To work embroidery yourself is a prediction of personal happiness.

EMPTINESS To dream of emptiness in something you expected to be full is a warning. Do not make changes or take on new challenges for a while, but save your energy for a more propitious time. If, however, you found yourself pouring from what appeared to be an empty container, the dream is a good omen indicating unexpected gains.

ENEMY To dream that someone you know is an enemy is a fortunate dream as it means exactly the opposite. You have faithful and helpful friends whom you may depend upon with confidence.

ENTERTAINMENT If you were entertained or at a place of entertainment, you may look forward to some joyful festivity and good luck in affairs of the heart. Leaving early, feeling uncomfortable or embarrassed during the entertainment, implies the loss of an associate or opportunity through your own carelessness.

ENVELOPE This generally represents obstacles in your path. A closed envelope denotes frustration — you must make more effort to be patient and calm. An open envelope means petty problems ahead. Keep your cool, don't lose your sense of humour and you will find that circumstances will improve.

ENVY To dream of someone envying you is generally taken as a good omen, indicating affection from those around you. If, however, you were envious of someone else, it may indicate the opposite. Romantic problems could be on the horizon if you dreamt of envying someone's looks. Envying someone else's possessions, on the other hand, may signal new acquisitions coming your way.

ESCAPE The classic dream of trying to escape with pursuers closing in on you is generally a symptom of anxiety. Traditionally, however, there are other interpretations. If there are troubles in your daily life, dreaming of failed attempts to escape indicates that they will continue. Escape from fire, water, serious illness or enemies, however, is usually a favourable omen of success.

ESTATE To dream of owning your own rolling acres is said to indicate a loyal and devoted husband or wife. Other interpretations take the view that a large estate suggests that you are trying too hard to compete socially. A more modest acreage predicts a steady but successful improvement in your circumstances.

ETIQUETTE It is not uncommon for people to dream of making embarrassing social mistakes resulting from an ignorance of manners. Generally they indicate a lack of confidence and undue worry about what others may think of you.

EVENING To dream of twilight or evening, especially a fine evening, presages pleasant, trouble-free years ahead in later life.

EXAMINATIONS An understandable subject if you are sitting exams though if that is the case the dream is not significant. An examination is, of course, a test – failing it in your dream indicates that you may be aiming too high in life. Passing it effortlessly can be taken as a straightforward omen of success.

EXPLOSION Old interpretations often indicate a relative placing himself or herself at risk. More recently, dreaming of an explosion has been taken as a sign of substantial improvements in your circumstances.

EYES To dream of strange eyes following you sounds disconcerting, but it has always been regarded as an extremely favourable omen. Fascinating or beautiful eyes which hold your attention suggest the love of those around you. To dream of your own eyes, which is more unusual – and particularly if there is something wrong with them – may be a warning that someone is working against you.

F

FACES The interpretation of the dream depends largely on the expression of the faces concerned. Broadly speaking, pleasant, smiling, friendly faces indicate good fortune, enjoyable experiences or a social invitation. Disturbing, ugly or horrifying faces may be an omen of some setback or misfortune. The faces of strangers are traditionally regarded as a sign that you will be moving house.

FAILURE Any dreams of unsuccessful attempts to accomplish something or of a feeling of failure are a contrary omen. They indicate that you will overthrow obstacles and achieve ambitions sooner than you think.

FALL To dream of falling is very common and suggests an undercurrent of fear or anxiety. Generally, the further you fall, the greater the setbacks you face. Falling from a great height indicates that it will take some time to overcome your problems, and to be injured in the fall may mean that some emotional bruising will result. The dream must be carefully interpreted according to your individual situation. It may indicate the end of a romantic affair, losing possessions or serious problems ahead in business.

FAME Dreaming that you are a celebrity or being idolized by a crowd concerns ambition and striving to attain certain goals. Dreams of fame are traditionally interpreted as a warning that you are aiming too high and must be prepared for failure.

FAMILY These dreams are very complex because of our intensely close, personal relationships with family members. Individual family members usually represent themselves in a dream so, for guidance, you must look at what the dream involves. There are, however, traditional interpretations which take the view that to dream of a large family indicates prosperous times ahead and an upturn in your fortunes. The family in such cases may be either human or animal.

FAREWELL Bidding someone goodbye is a good omen if the subject was a stranger. It signifies a new friend or relationship. If someone was saying goodbye to you in the dream, a house-move may be in the offing. The only negative aspect is if the subject of the dream was well-known to you. In this case the end of a relationship may be approaching.

FARM There are several interpretations of farming dreams. If the farm was yours – and particularly if you were working on it – the dream denotes financial success resulting from hard work. If the farm was run-down you can expect mixed fortunes. If, however, you were visiting a farm, it may be taken as an indication of good health.

FEAR A broad and complex dream theme which should be closely examined in relation to your personal life before interpreting omens. Traditionally, dreams about fear are seen as a guide to how obstacles will be surmounted. As a general rule, the future augurs well if you overcome your dream fears. Should you fail, and the fear remains, it can be taken as a sign of disloyalty by someone you considered a friend. Alternatively, if you dream of trying to reassure someone who is afraid it indicates that a misunderstanding will be clarified.

FINGERS Injuring your finger may be taken as a warning of an argument with someone close, which you will probably cause. To dream of an amputated finger indicates financial obstacles, while a bandaged finger suggests that you will overcome difficulties. A pointing finger, while more unusual, is traditionally an omen of travel or a change of house.

FIRE Any dream about fire should be taken as a caution, or warning of approaching trouble. How you escaped or managed to overcome the fire is an indication of how easily you will cope with coming problems. A fire in a hearth, on the other hand, is a sign of peace and fulfilment. Benevant, the astrologer, maintained that fire dreams were always welcome. 'Thou hast dreamed of fire, hast thou?' he wrote. 'Why, thou hast had a luck dream. It betokens for thee health and great happiness, kind relations and warm friends. And if a young dame, or lady and gentleman should thus dream, then that which you sigh for, crave and weep for, marriage, shall soon be yours.'

FISH Generally, to dream of swimming fish is a lucky omen. If, however, they are on a fishmonger's slab, the reverse may be true, and disappointment may be on the way. Conversely, really putrid or rotten fish indicate pleasing financial news.

FLOODS Like dreams of fire, these about floods may be taken as a yardstick of how you will overcome obstacles. If you escape from the flood, for example, you will probably win through without difficulty. The condition of the water is important, too – a raging torrent indicates a long, hard struggle, while calm floodwater suggests minor problems easier to overcome.

FLOWERS A dream foretelling great personal happiness and success. Throwing away dead flowers, however, should be taken as a warning to proceed with caution in your dealings with others.

FOOTBALL Watching a game of football is a warning to choose your friends more carefully. Playing football indicates unexpected money, perhaps in the form of winnings.

FOREST The meaning of the dream depends largely on whether you emerge from the forest. Being lost or hiding in a forest may be read as a sign of future gains or benefits. If you are frightened in the forest, be prepared for a disappointment. Eventually emerging from the forest signifies that problems will be temporary.

FORTUNE A dream of contrary – the greater the fortune visualized, the less you are likely to attain.

FOUNTAIN A gushing fountain, particularly one with crystal-clear water, is an auspicious sign of good fortune ahead. A dry or muddy water supply points to setbacks and frustrations.

FRUIT A sign that things are going your way, if the fruit is ripe and attractive. When it is rotten or bruised you will achieve your aims only with difficulty. A bowl of assorted fruit indicates unexpected wealth to a degree which may surprise you. *See* **EATING** for specific fruits.

FUGITIVE If you dream of being on the run, expect a disturbance in domestic relationships. Helping a fugitive to escape points to depressing news about money.

FUN Innocent fun or enjoyment which is not at the expense of others is simply an omen of good times ahead. If the fun in the dream gets out of hand, or is malicious, expect difficulties in business or serious problems in relationships.

G

GARDEN A dream garden in full bloom is a most fortunate omen, according to Franximus, '. . . All who dream this must rise to wealth and honour.' A peaceful, beautiful garden predicts spiritual fulfilment, while a neglected, unkempt garden suggests a thorny future beset with problems.

GEESE Cackling geese indicate hypocrisy; someone is pulling the wool over your eyes. Don't believe everything you hear and keep your own counsel. To dream of quiet geese, however, is a sign of better times to come.

GHOST To see a ghost in your dream and to feel calm and unafraid signifies your ability to cope with problems and overcome them. If you were afraid of a ghost in your dream you may take it as a warning that you are not reacting well and are being overwhelmed by difficult situations. Try to maintain a more detached attitude, concentrate on priorities and do not be afraid to ask for advice and help when necessary.

GIANT Dreaming that you are a giant is a warning against risk, speculation or a large ego — remember you are not invulnerable. Traditionally, a giant in your dream represents a powerful enemy or great difficulty. The interpretation depends largely upon your reaction. If you confronted a giant with boldness and courage it predicts that obstacles in your path will soon disintegrate.

GIGGLING Unfortunately, if you were giggling in your dream it is a prediction of financial or business embarrassment. Take immediate precautions – it may not be too late to avoid impending difficulties. If others were giggling in your dream you may look forward to some exciting social events.

GLASS Clean glass denotes a clear path to success and good luck. Streaked or dirty glass predicts uncertain prospects with difficulties to overcome. Completely obscured glass is a bad sign for lovers and indicates a disloyal friend. Broken glass means a change in your personal or domestic life. Stained, cut or decorative glass of any kind indicates an upturn in your affairs.

GLUE If you were using glue to make a repair then it is a warning that if you are not careful you may find cracks appearing in your financial affairs. Getting glue on your fingers traditionally indicates close friends. Using glue generally, for pasting, etc., signifies security in status and position.

GOLD According to the astronomer Ptolemy, 'To dream of gold is a dream of contrary. It is a sign of poverty and distress. Beware of speculations; it is not all gold that glitters. To dream that thy lover has plenty of gold denotes disagreement when thou marriest thy lover. Gold is often an omen of sickness or sorrow, as the results of bad fortune'.

GOSSIP Gossiping generally denotes domestic disputes or arguments over property. If you were caught gossiping in your dream you must take it as a warning to use more discretion if you wish to avoid embarrassment. Being gossiped about is a fortunate omen predicting good news.

GRADUATION Taking part in a graduation ceremony signifies a gratifying achievement, or promotion in business.

GRAIN Always a good omen, implying that your industry and enthusiasm will be greatly rewarded.

GRASS Lush green grass is a sign of prosperity, but poor, withered grass is an indication that you will have to work hard to achieve your goals. Planting or tending grass denotes security, though not wealth, but cutting and mowing grass forecasts sad or disappointing news.

GRAVE An unfavourable dream. Flowers on a grave indicate a broken promise. If the grave in your dream was neglected or open then it symbolizes some sadness. Seeing digging or being aware of your own grave denotes opposition or a strong adversary. Should you fall or stumble into a grave in your dream then you will lose a friend.

GRAVESTONE A happy omen. Old gravestones represent old friends you will meet again. New gravestones symbolize new opportunities for the dreamer.

GRIEF A dream of contrary: you will soon be celebrating and joyful.

GUIDE Whether you were guiding someone or being guided yourself, the dream implies that you will meet an influential person who could be of some benefit to you. Consulting a guide or guide book suggests a new opportunity in the near future.

GUN If a gun, or the sound of a gun-shot, features in your dream it is a warning that you have a hidden enemy, perhaps even someone you trust. The problem, however, is only temporary. If you load or fire the gun yourself, you could end up in hot water, brought on by your own inability to control your temper.

H

HAIR Luxuriant hair in a dream denotes continued health and prosperity. To dream that your hair is thin, split, coming out or turning grey is a sign of poor health, either in you or your partner, or of business and and career problems. Dreaming that hair is growing where it shouldn't signifies financial prosperity. Styling, combing or setting your own hair forecasts satisfaction, even success in any ventures you are involved in. If you dreamt of cutting someone else's hair you could lose a friend.

HALL If your dream featured a public hall then it denotes a lack of decision. A grand hall or foyer implies a change, probably for the better. An ordinary hallway indicates some temporary frustrations though a long and narrow hallway points to delay and anxiety.

HAM A good omen for the dreamer, signifying prosperity, good fortune and a happy family circle. Any difficulties will soon fade away and you may look forward to advancement in career and business.

HAMPER If a picnic hamper featured in your dream – congratulations. You have some harmonious and happy family gatherings ahead. If it was a full laundry hamper then you are entering an industrious but rewarding period. An empty laundry hamper unfortunately indicates some temporary upset.

HANDS Shaking hands in your dream denotes reconciliation or the welcome arrival of an absent friend. If you dreamt your hands were dirty you are in danger of being involved in something dishonourable or illegal – avoid this. The consequences of such an action would degrade and distress you. Clean hands, however, symbolize satisfaction, but if you were washing your hands then it is a sign of an uneasy conscience. A bandaged hand indicates some temporary setbacks, though swollen or gnarled hands predict financial gain.

HANGING Fortunately this is a dream of contrary, so if you dreamt you were being hanged you are entering a period of advancement and prosperity. If you saw another person hanged, then it denotes good luck to them. If you were the hangman it is a warning not to indulge in loose talk or criticism: it could rebound on you.

HARE A small group of hares in your dream is a sign that you have a close circle of good friends whom you may depend on. If a hare runs towards you, look forward to a visit from a dear friend. A running hare may indicate a change of address but a pursued hare predicts enemies and opposition – don't worry, you will outrun them.

HARP Harmonious music is always a good omen of a long and happy life. Any problems, such as a broken string or discordant sounds, denote troubles ahead.

HARVEST A fortunate dream and the portent of a prosperous period and happy achievements, bright social events and an upturn in business or trade. A rich harvest predicts success in all your ventures. A poor, unsatisfactory harvest indicates a lack of self-esteem and a feeling of being used or put upon. Do not allow yourself to be exploited. Be more self-assertive and make an effort to voice your own opinions. If you can do this calmly and without aggression you will gain respect and support and make more progress.

HASTE If your dream was dominated by haste and hurry it denotes anxiety and insecurity, possibly in business matters. You can cope better than you think, if only you will take time to plan ahead and to delegate.

HAT A new hat predicts success and achievement for the dreamer. A top hat is a particularly good omen and points to a rise in status. An old or shabby hat signifies some petty problems at work. If you lose or someone steals your hat then you must take steps to disarm a very determined adversary. Someone else wearing or putting on your hat is a sign that a rival is trying to supplant you or, alternatively, is claiming something which by right belongs to you.

HEADLIGHTS Headlights which are directly facing or moving towards you indicate a dangerous or difficult situation which you must take immediate and decisive action to avoid.

HEAT To dream of feeling hot or stifled is a simple warning, implying a passionate nature and a quick temper which is going to land you in hot water and embarrassingly difficult situations.

HEAVEN A significant dream which predicts a complete change of lifestyle. Although you may find this difficult to adjust to, persevere, for a dream of heaven signifies a peaceful and spiritually happy life for the dreamer.

HEDGE To dream you were clipping a hedge is a lucky omen, as is a neat green or flowery hedge, indicating prosperity and true love. A thorny hedge or one that is an obstacle to the dreamer predicts strong competition, hostility and rivals. You must be prepared for a period of difficulties and disappointments.

HELL An unfortunate dream indicating material gain at the cost of your health, friendship and popularity. Do not allow money to be your number one priority, for it could bring you enemies and your gains may only be transitory.

HERBS To dream of an aromatic herb garden is a good omen and denotes a comfortable, satisfying life. Specific herbs symbolize different situations, e.g. sage indicates wisdom and respect; thyme portends prosperity and good luck in love; wormwood predicts difficulties and disappointments. Poisonous herbs such as hemlock and aconite signify danger. Medicinal herbs are generally understood to mean recovery from illness. Smelling herbs and spices traditionally indicates travel to exotic places.

HERO If you were the hero in your dream then it is a dream of contrary and you should be prepared for a rebuke or criticism which will pierce your armour, possibly because you acknowledge it to be true or deserved. Don't worry, you can make amends and the situation is only temporary. If someone else played the hero in your dream then you may have an unexpected spot of good luck.

HIDE To dream you were hiding indicates an uneasy conscience and consequently you should avoid participating in anything you might later be ashamed of. If you were hiding something in your dream it signifies secrecy and anxiety. Remember a problem shared is a problem halved: get it out into the open and it will probably fade away.

HOLLY Generally a fortunate dream indicating a prosperous and sociable period. If, however, you were prickled by the holly you must avoid trivial tittle-tattle and gossip for it could lead to your own humiliation.

HONEY Like clover, honey is one of the most lucky omens, predicting domestic bliss, a long life, good health, independence and prosperity. According to Ptolemy, 'It is a notable dream, foretelling sweetness in wedlock, in the domestic and social circle, and sweetness in all secular pursuits.'

HORN To hear a car horn in your dream is a danger signal, so avoid risks and speculation. If you blew a horn or heard one then look forward to an upturn in your social life. If, however, the sound of the horn was very distant, you may hear from an absent friend. A loud repeating disagreeable sound indicates disagreements and disputes.

HORSE The interpretation depends upon the details of your dream. A noble or fine-looking horse in your dream is generally a good omen. If you were riding or sitting astride a horse there will be a rise in status for you. Falling or being thrown from a horse indicates that your plans may be thwarted. Seeing a group of horses is a sign of comfort and security. A foal in your dream predicts good news, though kicking or fighting horses indicate bad news. Racing horses will bring you almost immediate success. Grooming or seeing a horse re-shod is lucky for financial matters, as is a horseshoe in your dream, which also denotes amazing good luck. Traditionally a white horse means a marriage and a black horse a death or parting.

HURT To dream of being hurt is a dream of contrary, implying that you will achieve advancement in your career and happiness in your personal life. Any attempts to stand in your way will be abortive.

ILLNESS If you dream of suffering from some illness, take heed of future plans – they may not work out as well as you expect. If, however, someone else is ill, there is an ancient interpretation that a promise made to you may be broken.

INJURY Dreaming of suffering a physical injury indicates that someone is working against your interests, and caution should be employed. Something which endangers your stature or reputation is, however, a favourable omen, suggesting that your efforts will be rewarded.

INSANITY A classic dream of contrary, indicating good news and a successful outcome to plans. If the insanity did not affect you, but others, the news may not be as welcome as you expect.

INSECTS Generally an indication of obstacles and how you will overcome them. If the insects were troublesome and you succeeded in killing them, a satisfactory outcome is predicted. Should they, however, escape your attempts to swat them, be prepared for disappointments ahead.

INSULT Traditionally, being insulted signifies trouble or difficulties ahead. Other interpretations see it as a dream of contrary, predicting loyalty and support from those around you.

ISLAND If the island of your dream represented paradise, then changes, travel or even a house move may lie ahead. If, on the other hand, you were a castaway waiting for rescue, then you may encounter difficulties in business.

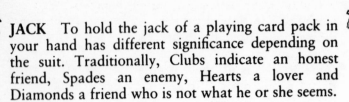

J

JACK To hold the jack of a playing card pack in your hand has different significance depending on the suit. Traditionally, Clubs indicate an honest friend, Spades an enemy, Hearts a lover and Diamonds a friend who is not what he or she seems.

JACKDAW An unfavourable omen of disappointment, or even depression. Old sources say that, if you catch the bird, your gloom will disappear.

JADE The traditional Chinese symbol of good fortune is a lucky omen in a dream. Prosperity lies ahead, though not without hard work.

JAWS Injury or pain around your jaw represents someone speaking ill of you, causing problems which will eventually be overcome. The jaws of others – human or animal – indicate that someone is willing to help you financially. A nightmare of being crushed between jaws may point to a relationship damaged through misunderstanding.

JEALOUSY A prediction of problems ahead at work or at home caused by dissatisfaction. If, in the dream, you were aware of someone being jealous of you, there may soon be problems with another person which you will have to resolve.

JELLY Far from being an indication of pleasant experiences ahead, dreams of jelly foretell obstacles or disappointment which must be firmly handled.

JELLYFISH This dangerous and unappealing creature is a warning to be on guard against hidden snags or problems arising from a proposal about which you feel doubtful. Proceed with caution.

JEWELLERY A particularly favourable omen for lovers, whether buying, selling, giving or receiving jewellery. If you dream of having jewellery stolen, you may expect problems in money matters. Recovery of stolen jewels suggests a settlement of financial difficulties.

JOCKEY Folklore and old interpretations claim that a woman dreaming of a jockey should expect a proposal of marriage. For a man, it is a warning to stick to a stable relationship.

JOURNEY A change in circumstances may be expected – whether it will prove to be favourable or otherwise depends upon the nature of your dream journey. If you found it enjoyable then the changes may be beneficial. If, however, the journey was uncomfortable then the transition may not be a smooth one.

JUDGE Dreaming of standing in the dock facing a judge indicates a period of trials and difficulties which will eventually be overcome. If the judge is sympathetic in your dream, then they may be resolved quickly.

JUMPING Jumping, especially over obstacles or hurdles, is a sign of problems which have to be carefully negotiated. Success will depend upon how much time and effort you devote to them.

JUNGLE A warning to economize if you wish to avoid financial problems caused by excessive spending.

JURY To dream of being a jury member is not a good sign and one which signals adverse fortunes ahead. If you dream of watching a jury at work, merely as an onlooker, then your imminent problems will easily be resolved.

K

KANGAROO Jumping kangaroos indicate travel for the dreamer. A mother with a baby in her pouch predicts an unexpected but exciting journey.

KENNEL If a kennel featured in your dream it signifies a person with whom you can make no headway. Your friendly overtures will be ignored and you will be happier if you give them up as a bad job.

KETTLE A shining kettle on the job symbolizes domestic harmony and contentment. A dull, cold or dry kettle predicts a period of financial austerity. Budget wisely.

KEYS A dream in which many keys are featured is a happy omen of brisk trade, business opportunities and achievements in your career. Finding keys indicates that any present problems are only temporary: you will soon find solutions and new directions to turn them to your advantage. Traditionally, to give someone a key predicts news of a marriage; to receive one forecasts news of a birth. Losing keys denotes disappointment and a broken key implies a lost opportunity. Turning the key in a lock suggest an exciting new venture and to be in charge of keys symbolizes a rise in status.

KILL To dream that you killed someone, either by accident or design, is a warning of difficulties that will test and try your temper. Keep cool if you wish to avoid making any disastrous moves or decisions. To kill an animal or bird in your dreams is a sign that there are obstacles ahead which you will overcome using your own resources and dexterity.

Should you witness the killing of an animal or bird, be on your guard against improper approaches, infidelity by someone you love or the end of an affair.

KING Dreams involving royalty generally signify happiness, prestige and dignity for the dreamer. If, however, there was embarrassment or an unfriendly atmosphere you could be aiming too high in your ambition and expectations, and you could be disappointed. Alternatively some malicious gossip could be the cause of your downfall –. keep your own counsel, do not confide in anyone for a while.

KISS Kissing a friend, a relative or a loved one in your dream is a sign of affection and happiness in your life. To give a reluctant kiss indicates a false friend, as in the Judas kiss, or alternatively, infidelity in your lover or partner. A kiss you didn't want to receive predicts some irritation or a minor illness for the dreamer. Kissing children or babies is always a good omen of triumph over adversity.

KITCHEN A dream relating to your personal life. A clean and homely kitchen indicates a happy social occasion or good news. A bare or messy kitchen is a sign of fatigue, so look after your health: you probably need a tonic to boost your flagging energy.

KITE Your dream kite symbolizes success. If the kite soared high and free you will attain your highest ambitions – luck is on your side. A damaged kite, perhaps with tangled or broken string, predicts disappointment and mismanagement. You would do well to review your financial and business arrangements personally.

KNIFE An unfavourable dream all round. A clean, sharp knife indicates a dangerous enemy who is capable of causing you pain or distress. A dull, blunt knife means hard work with little to show for it. A knife that has rusted denotes domestic strife and a closed knife warns of money troubles. To cut yourself with a knife signifies cash flow problems which could severely embarrass you.

KNIT If knitting is your regular hobby then the dream probably has no special significance for you. Generally, knitting is regarded as a peaceful, relaxing occupation which signifies domestic contentment and tranquillity. Fancy knitting indicates a change from normal, an interesting new friend or a visit from an old one. If your knitting got into a tangle or you dropped stitches then you may expect some domestic upsets.

KNOB Knobs, including door knobs, are a very lucky omen. Your speculations should pay off and you could be due for a small win.

KNOCK If you heard the sound of knocking in your dream, congratulations – it heralds the arrival of some unexpected money. If you were doing the knocking the dream implies that there is something unacceptable in your behaviour. Remember you are judged by the company you keep, avoid tittle-tattle and think hard about your life style.

KNOT A knot featuring in your dream signifies differences or difficulties with your partner or someone close to you. If you untied it then your cares will soon be ironed out. If it remained or you cut through it, there could be a serious rift or a complete break, if you do not take positive steps to arrive at a compromise.

L

LABOUR Labour in the sense of physical work means progress through your own efforts. To dream of watching a labourer points to increased prosperity.

LADDER In much the same way as dreams of climbing, a ladder generally indicates the ups and downs of success. Ascending a ladder is regarded as a favourable omen, while descent suggests pitfalls and problems ahead. Similarly, a high ladder means great achievements or attaining ambition. A broken rung represents an obstacle which you will overcome.

LAKE A lake symbolizes the way ahead, and your progress is represented by the condition of the water. If it is smooth, for example, you may expect steady progress in business or domestic affairs. If the surface is stormy or choppy then there may be problems which can only be overcome by persistence and dedication. One interesting variation is a lake by moonlight which points to great happiness in matters of love and romance.

LAMB A lamb symbolizes home and family life and is usually a favourable omen. To dream of taking care of a lost lamb, especially if you pick it up, predicts deep pleasure at meeting an old friend you have not seen for some time.

LAMP A dream of good fortune, depending upon the brightness of the lamp you saw. At its most brilliant it denotes success and recognition in your chosen field. The dimmer the lamp becomes, the gloomier the outlook – a weak light signifies disappointment or setbacks; an unlit lamp is said to foretell news of an illness.

LAND The meaning of the dream depends largely on who owned the land. If it was yours, the dream is a good omen for financial success. If you were a tenant and dreamt of being evicted, prepare yourself for disappointment. Any land transactions or change of ownership are said to signify a house move.

LAUGHTER Laughter has long been associated with romance in dream symbolism. The louder or more uncontrolled your laughter, the more care and attention you should pay to a relationship. The laughter of children indicates financial good fortune.

LAUNDRY Washing clothes, particularly by hand, indicates a strong association with someone which must be handled carefully. It could result in mutual benefits but, with thoughtlessness, may deteriorate into quarrels. To dream of visiting a laundry is a sign of a forthcoming celebration.

LEFT-HANDEDNESS If you are left-handed the dream predicts successful ventures. For a right-handed person to dream of left-handedness denotes minor setbacks which will easily be overcome.

LEGACY To dream of being left money is always a good omen – the greater the sum, the greater the good fortune.

LETTER Messages in dreams are sometimes conveyed in the form of a letter, which is generally a sign of news. If the contents of the letter were pleasant, then the news will be to your advantage. But if the letter was worrying, or of an official nature, difficulties may lie ahead.

LIES Much depends upon who was telling the whoppers. If they came from you, troubles may result from your own actions. Others telling lies may denote a new partnership.

LIGHTNING Lightning has always been a symbol of immense good luck which falls unexpectedly. But remember that it comes from a troubled sky – to dream of lightning also implies a period of stress or worry.

LION A sign of leadership, denoting honour or career success. A roaring lion points to problems resulting from the jealousy of someone near to you.

LIPS If the lips were a significant feature of your dream, try to remember the shape of them. Attractive lips indicate contentment in your love life. Thin lips suggest that you should not take others on face value alone, while dry or sore lips point to temporary ill health, or obstacles in the path of making money.

LOCOMOTIVE Sitting at the controls of a moving locomotive is generally considered to indicate travel, though some sources see it as achievement of ambition. Making a journey by train indicates a rise in income. Watching a train pass by is a sign of an unexpected visit from friends.

LONELINESS To dream of feeling lonely is another of those dreams of contrary – a sure indication of a busy social life ahead.

LOST Losing an item which you are particularly fond of is a sign that you may be overreaching yourself. Take stock and proceed carefully. If you eventually found the missing item, the problem may only be of a minor nature.

LOVE To dream of failing in love indicates, you may be relieved to learn, success and happiness with your chosen partner. To dream of being together with your lover is traditionally an indication of marriage.

M

MACHINERY To dream you were inspecting or working with well-maintained machinery indicates that your present ventures will run smoothly and your industry will pay off. Broken or rusted machinery, or machinery that is not working, is a sign of family discord or difficulties in trade and employment. Take care.

MAGIC A dream which foretells change and revolution in your life. Unfortunately one aspect of this dream is the unmasking of a friend whose loyalty is questionable. There could also be upheaval in your love life. Don't be alarmed if everything seems topsy-turvy for a while as the changes you will experience are for the best.

MAPS A journey, travel, change of residence, even general changes in lifestyle are indicated when a map features largely in your dream. The size of the map suggests the greatness of distance or changes. A coloured map predicts bright prospects, though a plain, dull-looking map implies that you should think carefully before making any major decisions just now.

MARKET A bustling market is an omen of plenty, domestic happiness and good commercial prospects for the dreamer. Shopping in the market implies a party or an approaching happy event which is cause for celebration. A dismal, shabby market which is poorly attended indicates lost opportunities and austerity. You must think more positively and make out a feasible financial budget to improve future prospects.

MASK A simple symbol of deceit. Someone else wearing a mask is an indication that there is a two-faced person in your close circle. If you were wearing the mask, then it is a more favourable omen, denoting your own eventual gain from a plan that was designed to exploit you.

MATCH Striking a match, matching accessories or making up pairs of socks, shoes, etc. is a dream of good luck. You may have a win or receive a rise in pay, certainly you will experience a boost in your finances.

MEDAL Seeing medals in your dream either in a case or on other people implies envy or vanity in the dreamer. Don't waste your energy in this way: direct it into more positive channels. Wearing medals yourself is a straightforward sign that your industry and persistence will be recognized and appreciated.

MEDICINE Taking medicine in your dream indicates temporary problems which you will have no trouble clearing up. Giving medicine to someone forecasts a period of extremely hard work, but don't be discouraged: there are rewarding results for you in the end.

MEND Darning or mending clothes in a dream predicts a new financial opportunity – take it. Repairing tears in other items, e.g. curtains, indicates a period of austerity. Indulge your creative skills to economize and don't worry: it's only temporary.

MERRY-GO-ROUND As a general rule, whether you were watching or participating in the ride, if the atmosphere was enjoyable then the dream predicts an upturn in your life. A sad-looking or broken merry-go-round indicates a period of frustration or disappointment. You must persevere, for new opportunities are around the corner.

METAL The interpretation largely depends on the type of metal and its predominance in the dream. Traditionally, gold denotes financial embarrassment, sickness or property problems. Silver forecasts disappointment in love or a warning to be on your guard against deceit. Copper predicts hard times and warns against travel. Iron is a good omen predicting a partner you can admire and whose strength will bring you both great rewards for your hard work. Lead is unfortunate, foretelling the loss of a dear one. Buying metal indicates financial prosperity and selling it denotes an improvement in your affairs. Molten metal is a bad sign and a warning to change directon: your present course will get you nowhere.

MILK To dream of drinking it, receiving it or actually milking a cow, is an omen predicting good health, prosperity and rewarding work. Goat's milk is a lucky sign regarding career or business. Mother's milk is the luckiest sign of all and indicates enduring happiness. Cream denotes a busy social life though spilled cream implies a loss you must try to avoid – do not speculate or take risks for a while.

MIRROR An unfavourable dream. Ancient interpretations generally agree that seeing yourself in a mirror indicates deceit by others whom you will uncover. You must be more discriminating, avoid gossip and keep your own counsel. To see others in a mirror is a sign of dishonesty among your colleagues. A broken mirror denotes sadness or troubles.

MONEY Most sources agree that giving, paying and lending money are all good signs indicating a comfortable financial situation for the dreamer. Receiving money is also a good omen and occasionally foretells the birth of a child. Finding money indicates an upsurge in business and losing it forecasts a win or windfall. Spending money in your dream predicts lucky profits, while borrowing money denotes a need to consolidate your assets. Counting or saving money predicts domestic harmony.

MOON A full moon is an omen of joy and perfect love. A waxing moon indicates new challenges and opportunities. A new moon signifies a lucky month. Soft or bright moonlight predicts domestic unity and a close family circle.

MOUSE Mice in your dream predict domestic upsets. If the mouse ran away or you chased it then the situation will only be temporary. A mouse running up your leg or getting in your clothes indicates misplaced trust: someone you know is talking out of turn. If you killed a mouse, you may expect some financial gain. Trapping one denotes news or visitors from a distance – not necessarily welcome. A mouse being chased by a cat indicates that you are being too passive, so assert yourself and do not let others make decisions for you.

MUSHROOMS A good dream predicting business and financial growth through intelligent application of your talents and assets. Look forward to improvements in your status and social life.

MUSICAL INSTRUMENTS Traditionally anything to do with harmony is a good omen. If playing an instrument is unusual for you, the dream indicates a happy change in your life. However, a snapped string means the end of a romance and a broken instrument is a warning to look after your health. Discordant music predicts problems and vexation.

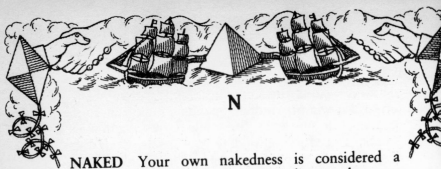

NAKED Your own nakedness is considered a fortunate symbol but it also indicates that any misfortunes you are currently suffering may be of your own doing. Generally, an increase in finances is indicated.

NAVY While it may be true that all the nice girls love a sailor, to dream of the navy indicates a stormy passage ahead in your love life.

NECK While it is fairly unusual for dreams to focus on the neck, there is a unanimous verdict that this particular region of the body represents an improvement in money matters. A broken neck, however, is a sign of marital upheaval.

NECKLACE Generally, a necklace in a dream is an indication of a love affair, or the end of a romance if the necklace has broken. In addition, you should pay close attention to the colour of the jewellery – *see also* **COLOURS**.

NEEDLES Any kind of needle, sewing or medical, has a potential for pricking the skin. If this happened in your dream it is a sign of disappointment in a love relationship. Threading a needle is a lucky omen, but if you had trouble in threading it, there may be obstacles in the way of your good fortune.

NEWSPAPER Unless the dream is prophetic in some way, the contents of the newspaper are less significant than the act of reading the newspaper itself. Dreams of this type invariably indicate news or events at a distance which will favourably influence you.

NIGHT If the setting of your dream was night-time, the overall indication is one of delays in future dealings. Other aspects of the dream should, however, be carefully taken into account. If the night was moonlit, the delays will not cause undue worry.

NIGHTMARE It is fairly unusual, but not un-known, for people to dream about dreaming. The general form is to have a nightmare but, at a critical moment, 'wake' from it to realize that it was only a dream while remaining in the dream state. Psychologically it can be an indication of repressed emotion. In traditional interpretations it represents the possibility of someone working against you.

NOISE Loud, discordant or disturbing noises in a dream point to upheavals in relationships with family or friends. If the noises brought you back to the waking state, it is a sign that any differences may be easily resolved.

NOSE The shapes of noses seen in your dream are of less significance than the condition of your own nose, which can indicate how your future will turn out. A nose bleed, for example, foretells a decline in business fortunes, while an injured or swollen nose is an omen of increased finances. A red or cold nose cautions against infidelity and a blocked nose is traditionally interpreted as a sign of a problem looming in your daily life.

NUMBERS The fact that you dreamed of a number, or were aware of a specific number of people or objects, should be taken as a sign of good fortune. Numbers said to be especially lucky are 3, 7, 9, 11 and 17.

O

OAK TREE A symbol of your personal and career prospects. If the tree is majestic and flourishing, the outlook is good. A young firm oak denotes years of success, but a tree without leaves indicates setbacks in business.

OFFICE Unless the office has some particular significance to you, it is likely to represent the romantic side of your life, rather than business. An unfamiliar office may indicate a change of partner. To find yourself in a worried frame of mind in an office may mean a strain on close relationships.

OPERATION Provided you do not work in a hospital or operating theatre, the dream signifies changes in your life and good news. If the outcome of the operation is not successful, the news may not be as encouraging as it first appears. To watch an operation performed indicates news which will take you by surprise.

OVERBOARD Unless you happen to work on boats or on the water in some way, falling overboard generally points to a disappointment or misfortune. However, if all ended well in the dream, the obstacles will only be of a minor nature. Some oracles say that this dream relates specifically to financial affairs.

OVERCOAT Clothes often play a significant part in dreams. Several layers of clothing or an overcoat to ward off the weather suggest that you should take steps to protect yourself against mistakes made by others.

PACKAGE Carrying a package suggests a burden and the dream indicates that you need to share this problem or responsibility. Indulge in a little plain speaking – a problem shared is a problem halved.

PAIN If there are no physical or medical grounds for you to suffer pain, your dream signifies a new and advantageous event in your life, if the pain was general. Traditionally pain in the heart denotes a romantic problem; in the teeth, petty problems; and pain in the throat or mouth is a warning against loose talk. A headache indicates a shock or unpleasant surprise. Painful limbs predict embarrassment caused by your own carelessness and chest pains are a sign of financial gains.

PAINT To dream of using or seeing artists' paints is an indication of a change in your life. A dramatic oil painting featured in your dream could point to an interesting new challenge, but the muted tones of water colours would denote a creative but tranquil period. Painting furniture or woodwork signifies an active period, either mental or physical, with perhaps a rather introspective or secretive attitude. If, however, your dream involved the exterior painting of a building, there is some news or a revelation in the offing.

PANDA This delightful Chinese bear is an omen of comfort and optimism. If you stop worrying then your troubles will just fade away.

PAPER As you can imagine, new paper indicates opportunity and a chance to prove yourself. Your efforts and industry will enhance your reputation and earn respect. Waste paper is also considered to be a sign of challenge and opportunity but it is up to you to take advantage of it. Coloured paper should be interpreted in relation to the meaning of the specific colour – *see* COLOURS.

PARALYSIS Ascertain that paralysis in your sleep has not arisen because of a physical problem. Total paralysis in a dream, whether your own or someone else's, suggests emotional upset or sexual inhibition. Partial paralysis is generally interpreted as a fear of impotency, rigidity or latent homosexuality. However, paralysis may also occur as a result of anxiety, or an overwhelming feeling of responsibility which you need to escape from. Give yourself some time to analyse your problem. If you are a generally inhibited person, try to loosen up, take advice from someone you trust or see a psychotherapist. Sometimes just talking through a problem with a sympathetic listener can help to put it into perspective.

PARENTS Obviously you must recognize and take into account your own attitude to your parents when attempting to interpret this dream. If the parent is deceased then his or her appearance in your dream indicates an important event or news. Traditionally, mothers signify love, security, comfort and generally represent your personal life. Fathers are associated with career, business and financial matters. In-laws in your dream imply a situation which could demand discretion and diplomacy.

PASSENGER Dreaming of being a passenger in a car or train predicts that you are on your way in life. Whatever it is you have been striving for is almost at hand. To dream of being a passenger at sea or in the air, etc., indicates a desire to escape from anxiety or worry. Take a break to restore your energy.

PEACOCK This exotic-looking bird in your dream implies a fine top show with little substance to support it. You must be sure that you can deliver before you commit yourself to any business or career responsibilities. Beware of overconfidence and arrogance – they could be your undoing.

PEARLS Generally a very favourable omen signifying good luck and advancement in all aspects of your life. If the pearls in your dream were strung together and the string broke then the luck is diluted somewhat. If, however, you managed to gather them up again you will find only minor and temporary problems in your path.

PERFUME A pleasing perfume, whether you used it or smelled it, is a good sign for business, career and romance. An overwhelming or pungent perfume predicts a passionate affair, a new love, an exciting sex life. A delicate, light fragrance implies a tender relationship or romance.

PIANO As with all musical instruments in dreams, playing or hearing a piano played well denotes harmony, successful achievement or good financial prospects for the dreamer. Discord, however, indicates problems and setbacks. Moving a piano is a sign of progress through your own determination. Tuning or hearing a piano tuned predicts some happy news.

PIGEON Flying pigeons herald important news from a distance. Feeding pigeons predicts some preoccupation with financial affairs on the horizon. Seeing pigeons walking about indicates domestic squabbles, but a pigeon sitting on your window sill is a forecast of romance.

PINS A dream of pins forecasts many minor upsets concerning family and friends. Being pricked by a pin is a sign that you will be asked to help someone, though sitting on a pin means a pleasant surprise for you. If you need to hold up a hem or make a temporary repair with pins, look out for a situation which could be socially embarrassing. A full pin-cushion is a sign of happy progress and satisfying achievement. An empty pincushion signifies a venture that will not pay off. Turn your talents to something more worthwhile.

PLANTS As long as they are healthy specimens, a dream of indoor or outdoor plants augurs well for any ventures you are involved in, especially if the plants are flowering. Sickly or wilting plants indicate that you must take more care and pay attention to detail to avoid failure. Tending plants is an omen of domestic contentment and financial comfort.

POCKETS Finding something in your pocket pre-dicts a happy surprise, probably an event you might dread which will turn out better than you could have hoped. A hole in your pocket warns of mortification or embarrassment due to your own carelessness. A dream which featured pockets, the contents or lack of contents being unknown to you, foretells of a tight-fisted colleague whose mean attitude will irritate you.

POLICE A policeman in your dream is a symbol of service and security. You will receive an offer of help from an unexpected quarter.

POND As in all dreams involving water the interpretation largely depends on the appearance and condition of the water. A pretty pond or garden pool is an omen of tranquillity and happiness. A swimming pool predicts a surge of social activity but if dirty, unkempt or empty warns against speculation and wasteful pursuits.

POSTMAN As you might expect, this chap's appearance in your dream is a symbol of imminent news.

PRIDE A dream of contrary, meaning that if your dream involved your own pride you may soon be humbled. Take a more modest view of yourself and watch your back. The pride of others in your dream indicates a promotion or reward for you.

PRINCE/PRINCESS A dream symbol which predicts honour, a rise in status, or promotion to a high position. However, your delight will be tempered by problems with your contemporaries who may try to use you. Be on your guard against sycophants.

PUB A dream in which you are the publican is not a favourable omen and implies you may find yourself under stress and pressure to act against your own principles. Maintain a steady head and use your own judgement. To dream you were drinking in a pub as a customer indicates financial reverses – you should try to economize.

PURSE Losing your purse in a dream indicates disappointment in someone close to you. Finding a purse is the sign of unexpected money.

PUSH Pushing anything in your dream predicts a happy outcome to your ventures or problems. Your own determination and strength of will should enable you to forge ahead.

PYRAMID This symbol in your dream signifies an exciting change of direction or some foreign travel. If the pyramid was not perfectly symmetrical and upright, it denotes irregularity: family or money problems could arise.

Q

QUARRELS A dream of contrary indicating harmony in your affairs, particularly in the sphere of work. Quarrelling with a stranger, according to some sources, points to a change of address in the not too distant future.

QUARRY This is regarded as a dream representing obstacles in your path. Tread cautiously, particularly if you found yourself in a quarry in your dreams — there will be pitfalls ahead.

QUEEN A favourable omen — *see also* **KING, PRINCE/PRINCESS**.

QUEUE To dream of waiting in a queue indicates that your patience or persistence will be rewarded, perhaps in a way which you least expect.

QUICKSAND A nightmare of sinking in quicksand should be taken as a warning not to be tempted by a glamorous exterior — whether in business proposals or people.

QUILT To dream of lying in a bed beneath a sumptuous quilt denotes material success. A patchwork quilt suggests that honest efforts will be rewarded. The more luxurious and comfortable the quilt, the greater the benefits coming your way.

R

RACE, RACEHORSE To dream of a race is an indication of your progress in life. Try to remember how hard your efforts were to win. Did you succeed, or lose? The outcome will point to how smooth your life will be in the immediate future. Dreaming of a racehorse is usually taken as a warning against speculation. If it turns out to be a precognitive dream of a future winner, exercise caution: it is no guarantee that you will win a fortune.

RAIN A downpour can put the damper on your dream, as it can in real life. You should take it as a warning of approaching problems against which you should take steps to protect yourself. Some sources claim that to be soaked to the skin in a torrential storm is a sign of future prosperity.

RAINBOW A wonderfully favourable symbol predicting that events will turn in your favour, bringing a happy outcome and great benefits.

RATS Any dream of rats suggests that someone is working against you, either by gossip, disloyalty or ruthless rivalry. White rats, however, are a sign that your present worries may be unfounded.

RELIGION Curiously, dreams of priests, nuns or anything connected with religion are an indication of minor problems on the horizon. To experience a spiritual feeling in a dream is, however, an omen of contentment.

RESTAURANT Most oracles associate restaurant dreams with financial fluctuations, but there is a school of thought linking them with health. Whichever you instinctively feel is correct, the general rule is that the more expensive the restaurant, the greater your prosperity or health. However, if the establishment was beyond your means, giving rise to anxiety, take care not to overreach yourself.

REVOLVER A warning of temporary problems (*see also* **GUN**). One oracle, it should be noted, saw revolvers as a specific omen of misfortune in travelling on water.

RIBBON The colour of the ribbon is, of course, important (*see* **COLOURS**). In general the dream carries the promise of an enjoyable social outing. If the ribbons are in profusion, be cautious about an impetuous love affair.

RIDING If you are riding a horse and are in complete control, the dream indicates good fortune. Should the horse bolt, or even unseat you, then be prepared for hasty action from a partner.

RIVER To dream of a peaceful river is a sign of untroubled times ahead. Otherwise, the state of the water is significant. *See also* **LAKE, OVERBOARD**.

ROOM Strange rooms often linger in the dreamer's memory. How they are furnished may be important. If you found the room generally pleasing it can be taken as a sign of coming success, often when it appears most unlikely.

RUNNING Running, or more specifically, running away from something or someone, is a common dream image. Being persued may denote anxiety or a lack of confidence. Failing to reach your goal through injury or tiredness could be a warning that you are overreaching yourself. Running successfully is a good omen, pointing to achievement in business or personal relations.

SADDLE This is quite literally a dream concerning matters which you regard as closest to you. Therefore any problems or discomfort regarding a saddle indicate that you take precautions before embarking on a plan of action. To ride bareback, without a saddle, suggests that your health or finances may suffer through carelessness.

SAILING Like other dreams concerning water, the sea-state signifies your prospects. The act of sailing, or controlling a boat, points to a realization of your ambitions. A small boat suggests great success.

SHIP Like all forms of dream transport, the ship is a symbol of your progress in life. If the voyage is smooth, there are few obstacles ahead; if the ship should sink, prepare yourself for trouble. Pay particular attention to the state of the sea and the weather in your dream.

SIGNPOST Quite literally a pointer in the right direction. A signpost indicates new directions, suggesting that some advice may be worth listening to.

SINGING If you were singing in the dream it is a sign that current difficulties are moving away and the future looks brighter. To listen to others singing, particularly if you find it grating or irritating, indicates trouble resulting from the actions of those around you.

SNAKE There is little disagreement among the oracles about this unpleasant symbol. The snake is traditionally seen as an omen of treachery, serious obstacles or someone working to undermine your efforts. Great care should be taken to ensure that you emerge from your troubles intact. The snake can also be a phallic symbol, cautioning against entanglement in an affair which you may not wish to prolong.

SPIDERS Irrespective of any fear you may have of them, spiders are a token of good luck or good news, particularly in matters of money.

STAIRS Like ladders, or any dreams of climbing, stairs indicate good fortune if you are ascending, and the reverse if descending. To fall downstairs is a warning to exercise caution in affairs of the heart.

STEEPLE A dream indicating that prosperity may yet be some way off, but can be achieved with effort. To climb a steeple is a favourable omen in the manner of all climbing dreams. *See also* **STAIRS, LADDER.**

STRANGERS Universally acknowledged as a dream of contrary signifying the love and loyalty of close friends.

STREETS Wandering in unfamiliar streets is an exciting omen of profitable new ventures, travel and new contacts.

STUMBLE To trip or stumble denotes an obstacle in your path. To fall means problems ahead which require your attention to resolve.

SUNRISE The dawn of new schemes, hopes and plans which, with some effort, will come to fruition.

SWIMMING To dream of swimming, particularly towards the shore, indicates that your efforts will be rewarded. You must obviously take into account the weather and state of the water.

T

TABLE There can be various meanings depending on the setting but, generally, a dining table indicates new friends and a kitchen table a need for renewed effort at work.

TAILOR Watching a tailor at work in your dream could mean an unexpected journey. This dream was traditionally regarded as an unfavourable omen for a young girl, indicating that she would marry beneath her station. To dream of tailoring yourself is a sign to guard your tongue.

TEA Pouring yourself a cup of tea forecasts a delightful discovery or surprise. Drinking tea predicts a pleasant social occasion and good company. If tea leaves featured in your dream they are the fore-runners of many little hitches or problems. Keep a clear mind and they will soon dissipate.

TEACHER If you were being taught in the dream it implies that you may feel irritated or patronized by someone in the near future. A dream in which you were the teacher suggests that you will reluctantly be forced to take sides in a forthcoming dispute.

TELEGRAM The dream is best interpreted according to the message on the telegram. If the information was good it predicts a windfall, a win or a financial coup. Unexciting or bad news in the telegram is a warning to curb your financial outlay.

THRONE The interpretation depends on how you regard your present status. If you consider yourself to be of a high social standing already then it is a dream of contrary and predicts a fall in status. On the other hand if you consider yourself as a person of average or low social standing, it signifies a rise in status or a position of authority in the community.

TOMATOES However they are presented in your dream they are a good luck symbol. Whatever your present ventures or plans, you should push ahead with enthusiasm, for tomatoes traditionally indicate success and personal happiness.

TRAFFIC Driving through traffic can only be interpreted by analysing your feelings in the dream. A smooth comfortable drive signifies domestic or family harmony, a period during which you will have a smooth ride through life. Watching traffic denotes a feeling of isolation, possibly because of a problem that is preoccupying you. Find someone you can share it with; now is not the time for you to try to cope alone. Being in a traffic jam suggests that you will be up against an obstacle which will require a great deal of patience. Don't let delays get you down – try to do something positive in the meantime.

TREASURE Finding treasure in your dream is an omen of imminent prosperity, a windfall or a legacy perhaps. Digging for treasure is traditionally interpreted as a welcome sign of recovery from illness. A surprising and valuable gift or bequest is predicted if you were diving for treasure in your dream.

TWINS Adult twins in a dream predict double trouble, then double joy. *See also* **BABY**.

U

UGLINESS To feel that you are ugly in a dream implies a lack of social confidence. Seeing yourself as ugly is a good excuse for not trying to be friendly and outgoing. The dream is warning you that to have friends you must first of all make the effort to be a friend yourself. A dream in which you see an ugly person is a sign of good luck for the dreamer.

UNDERTAKER This rather formidable person is actually a symbol of happy news, a birth or a wedding.

V

VIRGIN MARY In the past the religiously inclined have received great comfort from dreams of the Virgin Mary. She has always been considered an omen of peace and happiness – but one which should be tempered with caution as you should review the intentions of your associates closely.

VOLCANO A dream indicating too much carelessness on your part in the recent past. By overlooking the feelings of those around you, disagreement could result.

W

WALK A pleasant stroll, or any kind of leisure walk, denotes peace of mind and a worry-free passage through financial affairs. If you used a walking stick in the dream, there may be some assistance from others over minor problems.

WALLET Losing your wallet, on one level, is a straightforward dream of anxiety over money matters. On another it signifies a problem which you least expected.

WALLS Walls can either protect you or stand in your way. If the latter was the case, the dream represents obstacles which must be overcome through your own efforts.

WASPS These unpredictable little creatures represent someone you count on as a friend who is not as trustworthy as you would imagine.

WEDDING There are three distinct schools of thought about wedding dreams. One is the direct omen of an impending marriage. The oldest oracles denote looming trouble, while others indicate a short-lived period of good fortune approaching.

WHEELS Wheels are usually a dream symbol of progress through your own efforts. Whatever form they take suggests that you will shortly benefit in some way, perhaps even from an unexpected gift.

WINDOW Looking through a window is a sign of an active social life ahead. If you break a window in a dream there may be new friends and a change of address.

X

X-RAYS An omen of contrary indicating improved health. To study your own X-rays is a sign that you should reassess recent actions.

Y

YACHT As with all water dreams much depends upon the state of the sea. Most sources agree, however, that a yacht indicates a realization of financial ambitions.

YAWN A symbol of small significance, denoting small problems due to inertia or a lack of positive action.

Z

ZEBRA A tame zebra, and especially one eating from your hand, is a favourable omen. Zebras in general, however, suggest energy wasted on worthless projects and ideas.

ZOO Zoos, in the sense of a pleasurable day out, indicate travel and new contacts. If there was any sense of imprisonment or restriction in your dream, you are keeping too many problems to yourself — confide more in your partner or a good friend.